THE LANGUAGE ARTS HANDBOOK: A Total Communication Approach

Joanne C. Greenberg *received a bachelor's degree from Towson State University and an M.Ed. in classroom teaching from Loyola College of Baltimore. Ms. Greenberg has taught many levels of elementary students in both private and public schools. After leaving teaching to write, her contact with students has continued as a volunteer teacher. Ms. Greenberg is the author of over thirty instructional materials. She also does consultant work and is a part-time instructor at Western Maryland College. Married to Sheldon Greenberg, she lives in Ellicott City, Maryland, and is currently working toward a doctorate in education at the University of Maryland.*

Dr. McCay Vernon *is a psychologist who has attained international prominence as a writer and researcher on the psychological aspects of deafness. Even more important, his marriage to a deaf woman and his years as a teacher, clinician, and member of the deaf community give a depth to his other book,* They Grow in Silence, *which exceeds that of other publications on deafness. As editor of the* American Annals of the Deaf, *author of over 200 articles and books, and collaborator in the Michael Reese Hospital research on deafness and mental illness, Dr. Vernon's work has contributed to better programs for deaf children all over the world. He is Professor of Psychology at Western Maryland College and held the Powrie Doctor Chair in Deaf Studies at Gallaudet College during part of the writing of this book.*

Jan Hafer DuBois *received her B.A. in secondary education from Shepherd College, Shepherdstown, West Virginia and her M.Ed. in deaf education from Western Maryland College, Westminster, Maryland. She has taught deaf children at the preschool, elementary, and high school levels in both residential and public schools. For the last several years she has been engaged in an experimental program that uses signing and fingerspelling to improve skills in learning-disabled children. She is currently employed by the Maryland School for the Deaf in the Pre-school Parent Counseling Program. She lives in Shepherdstown with her husband, Keith.*

Jan C. McKnight *has a B.S. from Michigan State University and is currently furthering her formal education at Wright State University. She has taught elementary school for seventeen years, the last nine in learning disability classrooms. She has been using sign language in her room, extensively, for the last three years. Her interest in sign language was originally sparked by her sister-in-law, who was educated at the Ohio School for the Deaf. Mrs. McKnight is married, with three children and one grandson.*

THE LANGUAGE ARTS HANDBOOK: A Total Communication Approach

A unique multisensory approach to the language arts curriculum including lesson plans and reproducible student worksheets.

by
Joanne C. Greenberg, M.Ed.
McCay Vernon, Ph.D.
Jan Hafer DuBois, M.Ed.
Jan C. McKnight

with photographs by
Michael Taylor

University Park Press
Baltimore

A GOOD YEAR BOOK®

The illustrations in this book were taken from *The Signed English Dictionary for Preschool and Elementary Levels*, edited by Harry Bornstein, Lillian B. Hamilton, Karen Luczak Saulnier, and Howard L. Roy and illustrated by Linda C. Tom and Nancy L. Lundborg. We heartily thank Dr. Bornstein and the Gallaudet College Press for their kind permission to use these drawings in our book.

UNIVERSITY PARK PRESS
International Publishers in Science, Medicine, and Education
300 North Charles Street
Baltimore, Maryland 21201

Composed by University Park Press, Typesetting Division.
Manufactured in the United States of America by Eastern Lithographing Corporation.

Library of Congress Cataloging in Publication Data
Main entry under title:
The Language arts handbook.
Includes bibliographical references and index.
1. Language arts. 2. Reading. 3. Exceptional children—Education—Language arts. I. Greenberg, Joanne C.
LB1575.8.L34   428'.007   81-7598
ISBN 0-8391-1611-X   AACR2

CONTENTS

PREFACE

This book is for those who teach basic reading and language skills. Its purpose is to share the Total Communication Approach, a method that we and other teachers have found extremely useful and motivating in our classrooms and resource rooms. We have seen its potential for making the job of both teacher and learner easier and more successful.

The most unique characteristic of the technique is its ability to facilitate learning through the kinesthetic sense. The method is highly motivational even with youngsters who have not responded to other programs of learning or who have particular learning problems. The Total Communication Approach makes it easier for the teacher to meet individual needs. The method is easy to implement because it requires no additional preparation other than the information contained in this book and requires no costly equipment. The Total Communication Approach can be used in conjunction with any basal reader series or other reading program. Because of this and other characteristics of the approach, it can actually streamline some of the teacher's preparation and teaching tasks, and thereby make the reading program more efficient.

We have divided the book into five chapters. The first explains the method, the rationale for using it, and its application. Chapter 2 attests to the success of the method as revealed through research and clinical data. The third chapter is of particular interest to those teaching exceptional children. The next section is a practical application chapter that gives the details necessary for implementation and over 50 lesson plans, learning centers, instructional games, and other ready-to-use ideas. The final chapter deals with additional benefits of the Total Communication Approach such as its use in positive discipline and other classroom management. Also included are Student Sheets, which the teacher has permission to reproduce for classroom use, and an extensive list of resources.

Because the Total Communication Approach is flexible, the information contained in this book will be useful to teachers in many situations. The regular elementary classroom teacher will find that the Total Communication Approach and lessons can greatly facilitate teaching and learning of reading and other language arts skills. Those who teach exceptional children (gifted, learning disabled, mentally retarded, aphasic, etc.) will find that the approach can bring success to many who have previously failed in the language arts area. Additionally, those who are teaching basic skills to illiterate adults will easily see the advantages of using the Total Communication Approach.

This book was written amid the encouragement and assistance of many others who have seen the benefits of the Total Communication Approach and want teachers to know about these benefits. We would like to thank Judy Harkins, Anne Silverman, and Sandy Siger for believing in the book from its beginning. We recognize the help of Ellen O'Brien of Arizona State University, Fred Jacobs, Kathy Pannell, Beth Anderson, Diane Kratz, and Jim Durst who shared data from various studies in which they were involved. We thank Dr. Joan Coley, Paula Ottinger, and Dr. Hugh Prickett all of Western Maryland College, Dr. Doin Hicks,

Vice President of Research at Gallaudet College, and Dr. Marlene Bireley of Wright State University for their assistance.

We realize the importance of the support of our families, colleagues, and local school systems. We are grateful to our students whose excited response to the Total Communication Approach made us eager to share the technique through this book. Finally, we thank Janet S. Hankin of University Park Press who said an enthusiastic "yes," to the book at the beginning and then patiently saw it through.

Joanne C. Greenberg

to Sheldon,
J.G.

THE LANGUAGE ARTS HANDBOOK: A Total Communication Approach

CHAPTER 1
THE TOTAL COMMUNICATION APPROACH

The Total Communication Approach to reading and language arts involves seeing words, hearing words, writing words, saying words, and feeling words. It also involves getting excited about language and feeling capable as a reader.

The purpose of this book is to encourage exploration and use of this technique for the benefit of all students.

The Total Communication Approach is defined as the combined use of gestures, signs, fingerspelling, speech, reading, and writing to teach and learn language skills. Most current language arts instruction (that portion of the curriculum dealing with communication processes of listening, speaking, reading, and writing) already involves combining the visual and auditory components of communication. Teachers are proficient at including these elements in their lessons. They are therefore, already prepared to use the Total Communication Approach.

Fingerspelling and signs are elements that are unique to the Total Communication Approach, and for this reason, must be explained in detail. This book focuses on showing teachers how to help children use the kinesthetic sense (sensation occasioned when a muscle is moved) to enhance learning.

Teachers who use the Total Communication Approach continue to use pictures and other visuals to help students see words. They still employ voice, tapes, and recording devices such as Language Masters to help children hear and say words. The new

skill acquired from this book is how to integrate these elements with the new aspect of "feeling" words. Signs and fingerspelling are the tools teachers learn to use to facilitate instruction. The technique does not require drastic changes in existing language arts programs, only the addition of a new element.

WHAT ARE FINGERSPELLING AND SIGNS?

A manual alphabet, an alphabet in which hand positions are used to represent each letter, is the basis of fingerspelling. Many letters, such as C, L, V, and Y resemble their printed equivalents. It takes approximately 20 minutes to learn the entire manual alphabet (Figure 1) well enough for use in this technique.

Fingerspelling (Figure 2) is using the manual alphabet to spell out a word letter by letter. While much of the Total Communication Approach makes use of fingerspelling, signs are also employed. A sign is "a hand configuration moving in a specified way with respect to a particular place" (Klima and Bellugi, 1979) to represent a word. Some signs are icons, that is, they depict the objects, actions, or concepts they symbolize (Figure 3).

In the lessons in Chapter 4, fingerspelling is generally used in teaching phonics-related skills. Signs are more often helpful in sight word reinforcement.

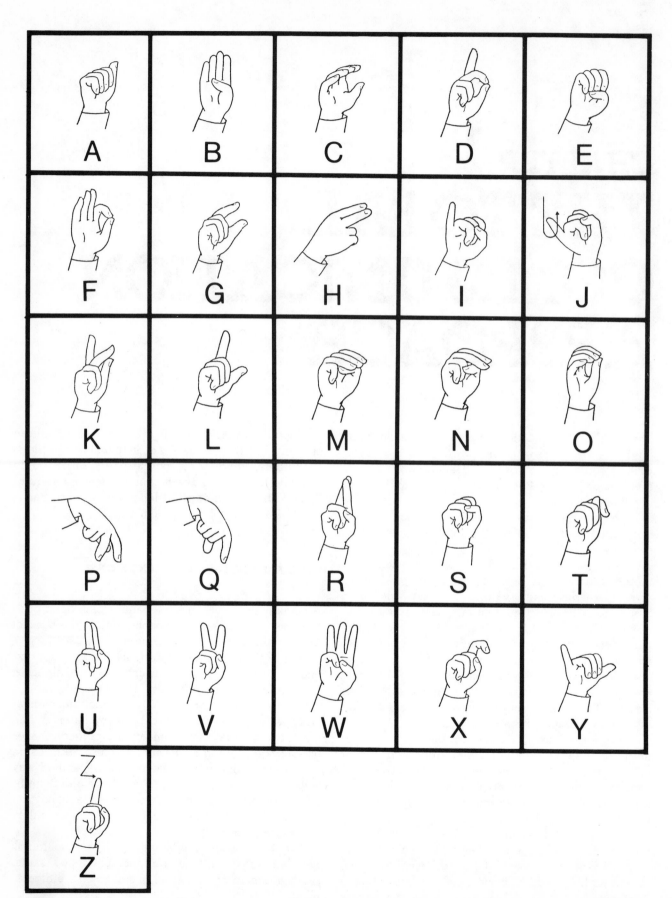

Figure 1. The manual alphabet.

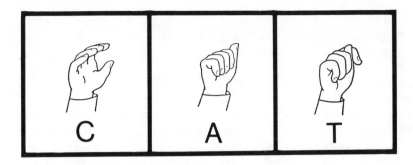

Figure 2. Fingerspelling of the letters "C," "A," and "T."

Professionals and deaf people use sign language extensively, and thus sign language becomes a primary method of communication for them. They logically would delve into the language much more deeply than a teacher who does not teach deaf children. Teachers may be interested in knowing for their own information, however, that American Sign Language (ASL) is the form of sign language used by the majority of the deaf community in the United States and Canada. It has its own grammatical structure and vocabulary. In other words, most people now agree, it is a complete language in the sense that Spanish, French, and German are. Other manual communication systems have been devised, such as Seeing Essential English (SEE) and Paget-Gorman, which are efforts to represent English manually (Bornstein, 1973). Cued Speech represents a third type of manual expression. In Cued Speech, certain hand positions are used in conjunction with speech in order to enable the "listener" to distinguish lip movements that are homophonous, i.e., that look like some other lip movements but movements but stand for a different sound.

The finger spelling alphabet in this book is the standard one used in the United States, and most of the signs are from American Sign Language.

butterfly
Hook thumbs palms in, and flap fingers.

Figure 3. The iconic sign for *butterfly.*

WHY USE THE TOTAL COMMUNICATION APPROACH?

Why use the Total Communication Approach? Use it because it is an educational technique that will add ease, diversity, and a motivating instructional method to a teacher's repertoire.

The Total Communication Approach can be used as one method of teaching and reinforcing concepts and skills just as drills, games, workbook assignments, and group discussion are used.

All good teachers are constantly looking for new ways to present and practice concepts. They are searching for methods that add interest and that might reach some of the children who have not yet been motivated in the language arts area.

In addition to being a good technique to incorporate among others, the Total Communication Approach has a unique combination of characteristics that accomplish several things at one time. The technique facilitates individualized instruction and is a multisensory approach. At once, it motivates, fosters success, and encourages independence. The Total Communication Approach is a valuable aid to the teacher in illustrating key language arts concepts. It also captures the practical teacher's heart because it requires minimal teacher time and no money (once you've bought the book, that is).

Added attractions may include visual memory, visual sequencing, fine motor skills, and decoding skills reinforcement that one teacher judged were the results of her use of signs and fingerspelling with students (Kelliher, 1980).

Individualization

Many of the activities suggested in this book involve an every pupil response to meet individual needs. For instance, one lesson involves all children in a group making sign language letters to indicate which vowel is heard in given words. In a matter of seconds, every child is being "heard" by the teacher. All children are actively and simultaneously participating in an orderly manner. Additionally, no one child is put in the sometimes embarrassing situation of being singled out.

The teacher in this lesson can see everyone's response and make mental or written diagnostic notes relative to children who seem unsure or confused, so that further help may be provided. All the children can be immediately reinforced by a statement such as, "If you have the same answer showing as Pat, you have the idea. Let's try another and see if more of you understand."

Children who are having difficulty with a skill will probably copy the responses of others rather than not participate. This modeling is advantageous in several ways. It provides immediate feedback by instantly giving the student the unknown response much as programmed learning or self-checking centers do. The child's hesitation is immediately obvious to the teacher who will then plan further reinforcement. This type of response, however, allows children to escape the embarrassment of publicly admitting they do not have the answer.

Additionally, using signs and fingerspelling helps students be aware of, and perhaps, be more proficient in alternatives to verbal communication. According to Stewig (1979) only 35% of human communication is verbal. The remainder of our messages are sent kinesthetically—by hand, eye, arm, and body. Children may benefit from encouragement to send and read nonverbal communication.

Multisensory Input

It is widely believed that using multisensory input increases the probability that a learner will acquire a skill or concept. It is not too difficult to provide visual and auditory input with most skills. It is more difficult to provide motivating kinesthetic input that is at the same time visual and auditory. The Total Communication Approach meets this need.

Many of the prepared lessons in Chapter 4 give step-by-step directions for expanding the multisensory approach to include the kinesthetic sense through use of signs and fingerspelling.

Some multisensory practices may become second nature to a teacher who becomes familiar with the Total Communication Approach. For instance, signs can be applied to new vocabulary in basal readers. A day or two before a story is to be introduced, the teacher can learn signs for half a dozen or fewer words that may be difficult for the class. (See Appendix A for names of dictionaries.) Whenever the teacher uses one of these words, she or he can sign as well as say them asking students to do the same. It has been the experience of teachers using this technique that students then know the words when they are introduced in print.

Motivation

Children are used to saying, seeing, and hearing words, but feeling words adds a new dimension. Almost without exception, students are enthusiastic about signs and fingerspelling. Youngsters are natural lovers of play acting and secret codes. They are thrilled to "act out" this new "secret code" in their school work especially if they have grown blasé about filling in the blanks, doing workbook pages, and playing sight word games.

One teacher reported that she was reading a book about sign language. The book, which had the manual alphabet on the inside front cover, was lying on the reading table when three children came for instruction. One of them started leafing through the book and became fascinated with the manual alphabet. The questions came from every direction. "What's this?" "How does it work?" "How do you make my name?" "How do you make your name?" and then the big one, "Could we use this to do our words?" The children's excitement indicated to the teacher the potential of the Total Communication Approach in teaching reading. The teacher then explored ways to include it in her instruction.

The teacher who decides to use the Total Communication Approach for teaching language arts has the advantage of using an approach that is totally new and motivating to children. Once exposed to it, they are eager to learn more and use it in new ways.

Illustrating Concepts

The Total Communication Approach is certainly not the only answer for teaching language arts skills, but it is a valuable technique for many skills, and perhaps, one of the best for some. Fingerspelling and signs are naturals for helping children understand the concept of rhyming words, opposites, and expressive oral reading, for instance. These lessons and others in Chapter 4 make easy work of some concepts that are generally difficult for children to grasp.

Success

Children who have trouble with language arts because they "can't sit still," or because it is so difficult for them, have been known to flourish using this technique. The Total Communication Approach encourages children to be active yet not chaotic. They do not have to spend inordinate amounts of time listening. They can actively participate in the lesson.

The Total Communication Approach can make language come alive for children who have previously not experienced success in reading and other language skills.

Independence

Using the Total Communication Approach fosters independence even when children are unsure of their footing because they are having difficulty or tackling something new. This technique can wean a child away from dependence on the teacher and encourage him or her to take steps toward becoming an independent reader.

Teachers who use the Total Communication Approach have had great success in prompting children who stumble over a word in oral reading. If a child hesitates, the teacher begins to fingerspell the word. In many cases, before the spelling is done the student will have the word out. Therefore, the child does not have to be told the word but just urged on a bit in many cases until she or he succeeds in recognizing it.

Teachers report that children who have been exposed to this type of prompting learn to self-prompt. One child was observed during an initial attempt at independent reading. As the child read, she pointed to each word with her index finger of her dominant hand. She came to a word which she did not recognize, although it was phonetically spelled, and she knew all of the letters.

She spontaneously changed hands, now pointing with her nondominant hand to hold her place and used her dominant hand to fingerspell the word. Although the teacher was watching from a distance and could hear the child whisper the sounds, she gave no help. The child immediately recognized the word, changed pointer fingers and went on reading.

Teachers who have watched children using fingerspelling to self-prompt observe that once the difficult words are learned, the children no longer have a need to use fingerspelling with those words, and therefore, discontinue it.

Efficiency and Cost Effectiveness

The Total Communication Approach fits teachers as well as children. One side benefit is that there is little or no preparation of materials for lessons which make use of signs and fingerspelling. Because signs can give everyone a chance to respond without using paper and pencil, some of these activities can be substituted for traditional written assignments, thereby lessening some of the teacher's paper correcting chores.

The teacher who wishes to try this technique can keep his or her wallet closed, for it is inexpensive to use. Other than this book, which explains how to get started, no special materials are needed. The main ingredients are a good language arts lesson plan and children's ears, eyes, mouths, and hands.

WHEN CAN THE TOTAL COMMUNICATION APPROACH BE USED?

Concerning the "when" of applying the Total Communication Approach to language arts instruction, there is not one right answer. This is a language arts technique for all seasons. It is useful in many types of teaching situations, from instructing one student to an entire class.

Large Group

Teachers can use the Total Communication Approach in whole class instruction. It is particularly effective for practicing basic skills that must be learned by rote. An example of this use is the lesson on homophones in Chapter 4.

The Total Communication Approach can also provide instant class tests. When a new skill such as distinction between fact and opinion has been introduced, children can be informally tested at the end of the lesson. For instance, the teacher can read some statements and direct students to show the manual alphabet "O" if the statment is an opinion, "F" if it is a fact. In minutes, the teacher can gauge the climate of the class to aid in planning the next lesson.

Small Group

The Total Communication Approach can be used in small groups to spark interest in a new concept. For example, letting children use signs to mime the action in verbs is an exciting way to introduce the concept of action words (Figure 4).

When a teacher wants to review briefly a concept taught earlier, the Total Communication Approach can be useful. Having the children respond manually to a quick oral review gives the teacher a chance to reinforce without the fuss and time required for a paper and pencil activity.

The Total Communication Approach is a natural for small group situations in which the teacher wishes to change pace by using an instructive game. Learning games which are already familiar such as Scrabble become even more motivating when adapted as described in the section entitled "Games" of Chapter 4.

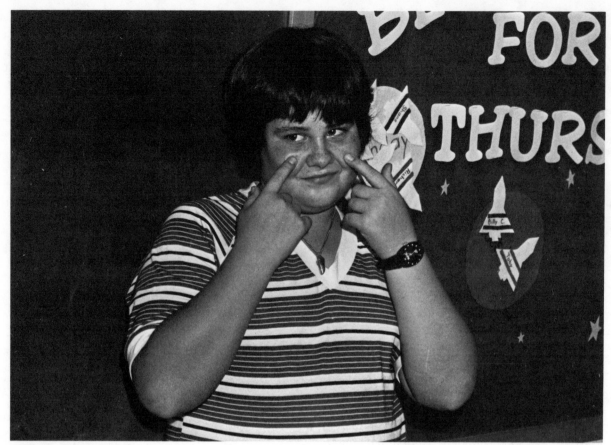

Figure 4. A student signs the word *cry.*

Partner Learning

Partner learning, assigning two children to help each other practice a skill, is an effective technique that can be further enhanced by the Total Communication Approach. Two students in need of initial consonant identification practice, for instance, can be given a set of picture cards and invited to find a private place to study. The children can take turns flashing cards that have the initial consonant on the back. The partner can make and say the sound for the manual alphabet letter to indicate the initial consonant. Not only will activities such as this motivate students but also facilitate learning by introducing kinesthetic input.

Individual Learning

One way the Total Communication Approch can be put to work for individual students practicing language arts skills is through Total Communication learning centers. As the "Learning Center" section of Chapter 4 shows, this technique can open new horizons for individual learning. The teacher who elects to integrate the Total Communication Approach into some of the class's language arts centers gives children another alternative to listening, reading, and writing tasks.

Homework

The Total Communication Approach does not have to be tucked in for the night when the dismissal bell rings. The benefits of this technique can go home with children as part of homework assignments. For example, students can be instructed to use the manual alphabet to practice weekly spelling words as suggested on reproducible sheet 12 in the back of this book.

The examples given are an appetizer to the long list of ways the Total Communication Approach can be used to facilitate language arts instruction. For each idea mentioned, there are many variations and tangents. The important point is that the Total Communication Approach is flexible. It can be put to work for students who receive the bulk of their instruction in whole class lessons, individualized activities, or a combination of these and other methods. It can be adapted to fit the needs of any class and the style of any teacher. The classroom does not have to adjust to the Total Approach. The Total Communication Approach adjusts to the class.

CHAPTER 2
THEORETICAL ISSUES, RESEARCH, AND CLINICAL EVIDENCE

The use of fingerspelling and signs in a Total Communication framework has great value in the teaching of reading and language. Extensive research and clinical evidence support this view (Bonvillian & Nelson, 1976; Chen, 1971; Creedon, 1973; Glass, Gazinaga, & Premack, 1973; Lane, 1976; Offir, 1976; Reed, 1971; Schiefelbusch, 1980, pp. 323-324; Vernon & Coley, 1978; Vernon, Coley, & Ottinger, 1979; Wilbur, 1979, pp. 261-264).

Although much of the research and theory discussed in this chapter relates directly to exceptional children, the findings have been successfully applied to children in regular classrooms, i.e., nonhandicapped students. For instance, the reader will see that the research dealing with gifted deaf preschoolers has obvious implications for normally hearing kindergarten and first grade students. Throughout the chapter, there is material that will prove helpful both to teachers who deal with the diversified needs of children in a regular class as well as those who teach only children with a particular handicap.

THEORETICAL BASIS FOR THE EFFECTIVENESS OF TOTAL COMMUNICATION

There are numerous rationales for why Total Communication is effective (Abbott, 1975; Asher, 1969; Asher, Kusuda, & de la Torre, 1974; Ferguson, 1977; Fristoe & Lloyd, 1977; Hoemann, 1975; Kimura, 1973; Siger, 1978; Vernon & Coley, 1978). They raise fascinating theoretical issues about the nature of human learning. For example, it may be that the brain hemisphere opposite that used for conventional auditory learning is involved in the motor/linguistic functioning of manual communication (Abbott, 1975; Chen, 1971; Glass, Gazinaga, & Premack, 1973; Goodglass & Kaplan, 1965; Kimura, 1973; Reed, 1971). Thus, individuals with left hemispheric damage, which often causes the loss of conventional speech and language, may be able to develop manual communication skills because motor function in most people is in the right hemisphere.

The explanation that is most readily apparent to reading teachers concerns the multisensory nature of the Total Communication Approach. Multisensory techniques are fundamental to most regular and remedial reading instruction (Abrams, 1968; Charuk, 1974; Fernald, 1943; and Segal, 1974). Feeling alphabet letters of sandpaper, tracing printed words, and handling three-dimensional letters are examples. The use of Total Communication involves the visual, kinesthetic, and auditory senses.

Corollary to the multisensory explanation is the demonstrated fact that when the reading process physically involves children they learn more efficiently and are better motivated (Asher, 1969; Asher, Kusuda, & de la Torre, 1974; Asher & Price, 1967; Creedon, 1973; Offir, 1976). Popular children's games such as skate boarding, hula hoops, hop scotch, jump rope, and others vividly illustrate the appeal to children of activities that enable them to use body movement. Such movement is intrinsic in the Total Communication approach.

When effective techniques also make learning to read fun, increase interest, and motivate, they are inevitably valuable. Children find Total Communication fun. In fact, activities involving it are often used as classroom rewards for students who have done well. Signs are vivid, dramatic, and fascinating, which makes them a powerful motivating force.

The ideographic nature of many of the fingerspelled letters and signs is another explanation for the success of Total Communication (Robins, Cagen, Johnson, Kelleher, Record, & Vernecchio, 1975). Many signs are actually "mimes" of the concept they represent. Similarly many of the hand positions of the manual alphabet look like the printed letter (see Figure 1).

Perhaps the most powerful rationale for the value of Total Communication comes from psychological learning theory, namely, the principles of classical conditioning. Appropriately used, Total Communication presents the reading stimuli to the child in visual, auditory, and kinesthetic modes simultaneously or very close together in time.

In Total Communication the sign (the conditioned stimulus) is paired with the spoken, or in some instances printed, word (unconditioned stimulus). This pairing is contiguous. Thus, the classical conditioning paradigm exists, but instead of Pavlov's meat powder and the ringing of a bell we have the sign and the auditory or printed word. If seen from the viewpoint of instrumental conditioning the sign serves as the S^D (discriminative stimulus) for an appropriate response, which is reinforced. These conditioning processes, which are integral to Total Communication, are fundamental to much or all of human learning.

The simplest explanation for why Total Communication works may be that signs (and sign language) are easier to learn than conventional language (Brown, 1977). For example, primates learn signs, and in the opinion of some, master elements of basic American Sign Language (Gardner & Gardner, 1975; Mayberry, 1976; Premack, 1971). Trainable level mentally retarded persons unable to learn oral language can use signs to express basic needs (Hoffmeister & Farmer, 1972).

Signs and fingerspelling do not require auditory memory and auditory processing. This may be another factor accounting for the method's effectiveness (Fristoe & Lloyd, 1977; Schiefelbusch, 1980, pp. 28-48 and 81-90). Corollary to this, figure/ground differentiation may be enhanced by this use of the visual mode. In other words, signs may be easier to distinguish from their background or field than speech considering that the context in which speech is generally used involves many other competing sounds. A problem many children have is distinguishing speech from background sounds (Fristoe & Lloyd, 1977).

Finally, with speech it is not possible to meaningfully sustain the phonemes indefinitely; that is, when pronounced very slowly, speech sounds often lose meaning. By contrast, with manual communication an alphabet letter or a sign can be presented at any rate appropriate to the learner. Fristoe's (1975) discussion of ways in which visual language may be easier to learn than auditory or written language is suggested for the theoretically oriented reader.

In sum, Total Communication combines every desirable characteristic of existing reading techniques. It is multisensory, motivating, and teaches by classical and instrumental conditioning. Along with its practical value to the teacher and child, the effectiveness of manual communication raises tantalizing theoretical questions about the role played by factors such as sensory modality, laterality, iconicity, and motor function in language and reading.

RESEARCH AND CLINICAL DATA

This section reviews evidence from studies on normal and exceptional children and adults. Most of the research was done within the last 10 years, indicating that the method has generated remarkable scientific effort in a relatively brief period.

Normal Children

Most new teaching developments in reading begin in classes with handicapped children and are then applied to nonhandicapped youngsters (Fernald, 1943; Myers, 1978). With some methods such as behavioral modification, the early work was done on animals (Skinner, 1938, 1957, 1968, 1971).

Similarly, with Total Communication, it has only been recently that the method has been used with normal children. *Sesame Street*'s efforts have been the most widespread. *Sesame Street* has used professional deaf actors to do fingerspelling and signing exercises as part of a reading readiness and reading instructional approach on television. What began as a few guest appearances by deaf performers using signs and fingerspelling has proved so successful that a deaf actress, Linda Bove, is now a regular performer (Vernon & Coley, 1978). Consequently, millions of children are receiving exposure to signs and fingerspelling in a reading readiness framework on *Sesame Street.*

Other data on the method come from clinical findings on children of congenitally deaf parents (Vernon & Coley, 1978; Vernon, Coley, & DuBois, 1980b; Vernon, Coley, & Ottinger, 1979). Because their parents use fingerspelling (and signs) at home these children are exposed to it even though they are not deaf. Thus, a sort of "experiment of nature" is created whereby the effects of signs and fingerspelling can be assessed.

The end result of the "experiment of nature" is that many normally hearing children of average or above IQ who have nonspeaking deaf parents read fingerspelling before entering school (Vernon & Coley, 1978). Fingerspelling is cognitively similar to reading printed letters (Klima & Bellugi, 1979). In fact, some read regular printed words because they are able to make the connection between the manual letter and the printed one (Klima & Bellugi, 1979; Vernon & Coley, 1978). Not only do these children read but they also write in the sense of using fingerspelling expressively (Figure 5).

This unique "experiment of nature" has implications for the teaching of reading to all children. It means that given Total Communication as a part of a reading readiness program, the early development of reading and writing skills would be greatly facilitated.

Additional evidence of the potential value of fingerspelling in teaching reading to hearing children comes from studies of children who not only have deaf parents but who are themselves deaf (Bellugi & Klima, 1975; Vernon & Koh, 1970, 1971). Many of them are fluent fingerspellers well before they even enter school. This means that like hearing children of deaf parents they can read and write (manually) before having been taught to do so formally. These deaf children learn this from a combination of fingerspelled words and signs manually communicated to them by their parents in the form of sentences; that is, they are not taught the alphabet as such in many instances. Even more surprising, they can "write" similar sentences to their parents, that is, they can fingerspell

and sign sentences. Once these deaf children enter school, they learn to read conventional print symbols more rapidly than other deaf children (Mindel & Vernon, 1971). In fact, many deaf children of deaf parents come to school able to read because their parents have already taught them to associate the manual and print alphabet to symbols (Hofsteater, 1959).

In stark contrast to the studies of deaf children of deaf parents are the studies of deaf children who do not have early exposure to fingerspelling or sign language. The reading level of these children is generally inferior (Meadow, 1968; Vernon & Koh, 1970, 1971).

Essentially what these findings on both hearing and deaf children of deaf parents indicate is that, if given only manual communication (fingerspelling and sign language), they read at a very early age. If speech were added in a classical conditioning framework such as is involved in Total Communication, learning would be even more effective.

Gifted Children

Total Communication has not been tried in a formal experiment with gifted children. The major use of the method has been in cases of gifted children born into families of deaf parents and/or siblings. These gifted children with normal hearing are frequently reading by age 3 or 4 years (Vernon & Coley, 1978; Vernon, Coley, & Ottinger, 1979).

In a unique experiment, a University of North Carolina audiology professor, David Holmes, and his wife Kathi, a former teacher of deaf children, started their newborn hearing son, Davey, on Total Communication. Now 2 years old, young Davey is beginning to approximate fingerspelled words on his hands. He has added words in his signed vocabulary that would not normally be present in so young a child's spoken vocabulary. The Holmeses also note that Total Communication has facilitated overall language and concept development (Holmes, 1980).

Most gifted children are fascinated by language and are highly verbal. Thus, Total Communication is potentially an ideal approach to early reading and language development for them.

Learning Disabled Children

An experimental program using the manual alphabet to improve learning disabled children's spelling skills was implemented in three resource room programs in Berkeley County, West Virginia in 1977 (Vernon, Coley, & DuBois, 1980a). Children chosen for the project met three criteria: they were classified as visual or haptic learners, they had poor spelling skills, and they

Figure 5. A deaf preschooler fingerspells her name to her mother as her mother fingerspells *yes.*

were all assigned to a second grade spelling text in the regular classroom. The county early identification consultant for learning disabilities administered a standard battery of tests including the WISC, Stanford Achievement Test, ITPA, and Bender-Gestalt to determine placement in the resource room and participation in the experiment.

The three resource room teachers volunteered to take four hours of fingerspelling instruction for teaching fingerspelling to their students using the phonetic method (Guillory, 1966). Instead of pronouncing each letter as a word was spelled, they said the word while fingerspelling, which is analogous to the "whole word" technique used in conventional reading instruction. This avoided a common mistake made by novices of fingerspelling who usually try to read fingerspelled words by individual letters rather than as meaningful units. By the end of the instructional period the teachers were fluent in fingerspelling one and two syllable words comparable to the ones found in the second grade speller.

The teachers were instructed not to introduce fingerspelling by the alphabet, but by starting at the beginning of the spelling text and introducing the spelling words by fingerspelling the word as they said it. At no time during the introduction to fingerspelling were the letters to be individually identified. Only ten minutes were spent on spelling every day. This approach facilitated high interest and guarded against the possibility of the success of this method being attributed to increased instructional time rather than fingerspelling.

All three teachers reported that the children were able to read and fingerspell the words after the third instructional period. When the first written test was administered during the fifth instructional period all of the students scored 100% except one. The spelling tests were first administered in two ways. The children were asked to fingerspell the words to the teacher individually and then a group written test was given. All of the children scored 100% on the fingerspelled test. The one not scoring perfectly on the written test was initially unable to see the connection between the fingerspelled word and the written word. Once the teacher showed her that what she fingerspelled was the same as what she should be writing, she scored perfectly on the remaining tests. After the first few spelling tests only the written test was used. A receptive fingerspelling test was also given. The teacher fingerspelled the words and the children called out the word which had been spelled. This test was given to the class as a group.

Some interesting problems and subsequent solutions were observed during the experiment. One child had particular trouble with the blend "ch" in the word chop. He first attempted to spell the word without using the fingerspelling and would spell cop. After the teacher encouraged him to use fingerspelling, he spelled the word correctly. Another child initially reversed the letters in a few two letter words. The teacher suggested he fingerspell using two hands, always starting with the left hand and the second letter being formed on the right hand. After practicing a few times with this method, he used only one hand and was able to spell the word correctly. One child would use two hands when fingerspelling. He would start with one hand and suddenly finish a word with the other. The teacher instructed him to use his dominant hand and to conceal the other. The suggestion solved the problem.

Walker (1977) also reported on the use of sign language with a class of reading-disabled students at the junior high level. These students used the manual alphabet to learn sight vocabulary. The technique was motivational and increased reading scores.

Mentally Retarded

Total Communication has found great success in the area of mental retardation with persons at both the educable and trainable levels (Fristoe & Lloyd, 1977; Hoffmeister & Farmer, 1972; Kahn, 1977; Mayberry, 1976; Richardson, 1975; Topper, 1975; Zweiban, 1977). With the latter it is obviously not a tool for reading instruction, but instead a means of establishing communication where little or none existed before. For example, many of these trainable level persons who are unable to develop basic speech for everyday needs can master the signs required for basic "survival skills." Thus, the introduction of sign language represents one of the major breakthroughs in this area of education during the last decade.

With higher functioning mentally retarded children both fingerspelling and sign language together, in other words Total Communication, are effective (Kopchick & Lloyd, 1976). The techniques are used both to help with reading and with basic communication depending on the aptitudes and needs of the individual involved. Two of Total Communication's major assets are the motoric nature of the task and the way the technique lends itself to games and activities (in contrast to dreaded pencil and

paper tasks). It greatly [...] motivation, and interest [...]

As far back as 1975 [...] providing speech and [...] retarded clients were [...] 1975). These 10% fo[...] communicate by si[...] speak for the first time [...] where speech developed sig[...] needed.

Aphasics

Once again some of the initial evidence on Total Communication comes from the field of deafness. It has long been recognized by teachers and others who work with deaf children that a significant number of these youth are aphasic (and/or dyslexic) in that they are unable to master printed or oral/aural language (Mindel & Vernon, 1971). Yet they are often fluent in sign language (Vernon, 1969). This rather remarkable fact has been seized upon by a number of speech pathologists and rehabilitation specialists who have generalized it by teaching sign language to nondeaf aphasics, including stroke victims (Balick, Spiegel, & Greene, 1976; Chen, 1971). Once aphasics master signs or fingerspelling, these communication skills are used to facilitate reading and speech. Results have been positive (Balick, Spiegel, & Green, 1976; Chen, 1971; Chester & Egolf, 1974; Duffy, Duffy, & Pearson, 1975; Skelly, Schinsky, Smith, Donaldson, & Griffin, 1975). In brief, the nondeaf individuals they studied who were aphasic, and therefore, unable to communicate by conventional means learned basic signs. This enabled them to make their wants known, and it played a major part in their overall linguistic rehabilitation.

Childhood Autism and Other Psychoses

In the field of childhood autism one of the few encouraging treatment breakthroughs that has occurred has been by the use of sign language (Creedon, 1973; Miller & Miller, 1973; Offir, 1976; Schaeffer, 1980; and Reed, 1971). Therapists and teachers have found that when all other efforts to elicit communication failed with nondeaf autistic children, sign language was often effective (Bonvillian & Nelson, 1976; Offir, 1976). Similar experiences have been reported in the treatment of very withdrawn schizophrenic persons and with one case of a dying child who reacted to his trauma with an almost psychotic withdrawal (Grinker, 1969).

ought blind children would seem to be the
ely to benefit from Total Communication
e it is an essentially visual modality. However,
ethod was tried by Mr. Jim Durst in the West
ginia School for the Deaf and Blind. He found that
ne kinesthetic dimension of fingerspelling was of
significant value in teaching reading. Also, some of
the blind children in his experimental class had learning disabilities superimposed on the visual loss.

For years fingerspelling and signs have been used
with students who are both deaf and blind. Those
familiar with the life of Helen Keller are well aware
of the success of the technique with her and others,
such as Dr. Robert Smithdas.

Deaf and Hearing-Impaired Individuals

Extensive research demonstrates beyond doubt the
value of Total Communication with deaf and severely
hearing-impaired children. It has doubled the reading
gains of these children (Vernon & Koh, 1970, 1971).
This is especially significant because children with
profound early onset hearing loss represent one of the
most difficult of all groups to teach reading and
English language arts to (see Table 1).

Table 1. Results of early manual communication

Investigator and samples	Results
Vernon and Koh (1970)	

32 pairs of genetically deaf children matched for age, sex, and IQ. Manual group had deaf parents, oral group had hearing parents.	1. Stanford Achievement Test Scores.
	  a. General average—Manual group better (1-4.4 yrs).
	  b. Reading average—Manual group better (1-3.9 yrs).
	  c. Para. mean.—Manual group better (1-5.7 yrs).
	  d. Vocabulary—Manual group better (1-1.9 yrs).
	2. Written language. Manual group superior at .002 level of significance.
	3. No differences in speech intelligibility, speech reading, or psychosocial adjustment.

Meadow (1968)	
56 deaf children of deaf parents (manual group). 56 matched deaf children of hearing parents (oral group).	1. Manual group better in reading (2.1 yrs). 2. Manual group better in match (1-2.5 yrs). 3. Manual group better in overall education achievement (1-2.8 yrs). 4. Manual group better in social adjustment. 5. No differences in speech and lipreading. 6. Manual group better in written language.
Stuckless and Birch (1966)	
105 deaf children of deaf parents (manual group). 337 matched deaf children of hearing parents (oral group).	1. No difference in speech. 2. Early manual group better in speechreading. 3. Early manual group better in reading. 4. Early manual group better in writing. 5. Early manual group possibly better in psychosocial adjustment.

Table 1 *continued*

Investigator and samples	Results
Montgomery (1966)	
59 Scottish children.	Exposure to, use of, and preference for manual communication did not negatively affect speech or speechreading skills.
Stevenson (1964)	
134 deaf children of deaf parents (manual group). 134 deaf children of hearing parents (oral group).	1. 90% of manual group did better than matched oral students. 2. 38% of manual group went to college vs. nine percent of oral group.
Quigley and Frisina (1961)	
16 nonresidential deaf children of deaf parents (manual group). 16 nonresidential children of hearing parents (oral group).	Manual group better in vocabulary, speechreading and better in education achievement. Oral group better in speech.
Hestor (1963)	
Deaf children in New Mexico School for the Deaf. One group had fingerspelling beginning at school age, one group taught orally.	Fingerspelling group superior on standardized achievement tests.
Quigley (1968)	
16 orally educated deaf children matched with 16 combined orally and manually educated deaf children.	Combined manual oral children did better in language, speechreading, and general academic achievement.
Quigley (1968)	
Rochester Method Elementary and Secondary Programs versus Simultaneous Method Programs.	1. Rochester Method student superior in: a. all subtests of Stanford Achievement Test. b. fingerspelling. 2. No differences in speech or speechreading.
Denton (1965)	
The academic top ten percent of deaf children ages 12, 15, and 18 from 26 schools for deaf. Manual group had deaf parents, oral group had hearing parents.	Mean achievement test score of manual group 8.2, of oral group 7.7
Morozova (1954)[a]	
Oral only programs versus Neo-Oralism (Rochester Method) Schools in Soviet Union.	Children with fingerspelling master in 2 years material requiring 3 years under oral-only method.
Brasel and Quigley (1977)	
Four groups, each having 18 deaf children. One group had deaf parents who used Manual English, one had deaf parents who used ASL, one had hearing parents and oral preschool training, and one had oral hearing parents and no preschool training.	Manual English group scored highest on all measures of achievement and ASL group was second. The two oral groups were last.

[a]This study reported by D. F. Moores in *Research on Manual Communication.* Occasional paper 7. Minneapolis: University of Minnesota, 1971.

However, the etiology of the deaf child's reading problem is different in major ways from that of the regular public school child or most other exceptional children. Thus these findings on hearing-impaired children do not generalize as directly to nondeaf children as does the other research in this chapter.

Other Exceptional Children

Many children with speech problems other than those already discussed (caused by aphasia, deafness, and autism) find sign language and fingerspelling tremendously helpful. For some it means that they finally have a means of communication in which they can do as well as others, a means of communication that can reduce the feelings of rage and helplessness they otherwise feel when unable to express themselves. For example, the severe stutterer can usually fingerspell and sign as well as any other child. This means that much of the stress of communication is reduced when significant others such as parents, siblings, teachers, and close friends in the child's life learn Total Communication. With the "safety valve" of manual communication to fall back on, the overall pressure of the need to articulate rapidly is reduced and speech per se improves. Similarly children with orthopedic involvements such as the cerebral palsied may have speech mechanisms they cannot fully control. However, there is often enough coordination in the hands and arms to make signs and sometimes to form fingerspelled letters.

With bilingual children there exists no actual research or well supported case studies using Total Communication. However, the theory exists for the application of Total Communication in teaching basic communication and reading to bilingual children. The logic of the theory justifies the effort.

CHAPTER 3
USING TOTAL COMMUNICATION WITH EXCEPTIONAL STUDENTS

The application of the Total Communication Approach to reading and language instruction with exceptional students involves first a thorough understanding of the method described in Chapter 1 and its application with regular students discussed in Chapter 4. These fundamental principles are applicable also to students with handicaps or other exceptionalities. This chapter adds to these basic techniques special adaptations for specific kinds of problems. In the case of certain handicaps, there have been many studies using the method. From these studies certain principles have been developed and are reported in this chapter. With other exceptionalities, the method has only been used in one or two experimental studies. In such cases, the actual parts of the studies describing the application of the method are presented in a way that enables the teacher to apply the same method.

LEARNING DISABILITY

One of the most difficult problems facing primary teachers who have children with learning disabilities

is finding effective techniques to use in teaching reading to these children who are not learning by the usual methods. It is generally assumed that a phonetic, structured approach is best, or at least that a strong phonics background is important for most children in order to fill the gaps when their sight vocabulary fails them. However, many of these learning-disabled students have difficulty linking the sounds to printed symbols, a basic skill necessary when using phonics as an aid to reading.

In order to show how Total Communication can help teachers of learning-disabled children, the actual reading program instituted by one of the co-authors, Jan McKnight, is described.

In her class, children are asked to use the manual alphabet for each letter or phoneme being considered. Applied in this way, Total Communication is an adjunct to a language-reading program.

In one of Ms. McKnight's experimental classes were ten learning-disabled children ages 7 to 10 years. Total Communication was used for 2 years. It was most strongly emphasized with two boys and one girl (ages 7 to 8, IQ's 94-105), and later with three additional children, all of whom had had kindergarten and 1 or 2 years of first grade. All had failed in a conventional program emphasizing phonics. They were reading at an early first grade level.

Their instruction using fingerspelling was in conjunction with the Merrill Linguistic Basic Reading program. The manual signs taught were only those needed for the words in lessons in this program. Thus, the teacher and students needed to learn only a few new signs at a time. In all other respects the lessons were taught very much as they had been in previous years, and for the most part, as described in the Merrill manual.

Since all three of the children with whom Total Communication was used were easily distracted, the ability to gain and hold their attention by using the manual alphabet was the first advantage noticed by the teacher. To ensure that children are paying attention, it is always extremely helpful to have them make some overt response. Teachers have, historically, asked children to point to the word or part of a word being considered or to read aloud the particular item. Having the child manually form a letter or sign had several advantages. The teacher knows immediately if the children are looking at the right place which could be in a book, on the board or just the teacher's hand. If they make no hand response, the teacher knows that they may not be paying attention to the lesson. If they make a letter sign unrelated to the word or letter being considered, the child might be paying attention but is focusing on the wrong material. The teacher then needs to help them find their places. Even though a child had the right place and was paying attention, sometimes the sign given indicated the letter was perceived in reverse, for instance, "d" for "b," in which case the teacher would make the correction by showing the child the proper hand position. Because the children faced the teacher, each could be quickly checked. Copying was at a minimum and was easily detected. It was impossible for a child to fake attention.

Once attention has been secured and correctly focused, the next task of the teacher is to ensure that the needed letter sounds are known to each of the children. If a new letter sound is presented, only that letter is displayed. The letter is not named, but the sound and manual letters are given simultaneously. The children respond with the simultaneous fingerspelling and sound. Repetition is natural. Usually the children repeat the sound and fingerspell it as many as ten times spontaneously. They often exaggerate signs, sometimes swinging the whole arm with each repetition. This is reinforcing and greatly facilitates learning.

Later, a new letter is displayed among a few known ones. As each letter is shown, the children fingerspell it and repeat the sound. Most often they repeat each letter about three times voluntarily before the next letter is presented. In this way, multisensory stimulation and adequate repetition are achieved with a minimum of distraction and a high interest level. The sound is paired with the visual stimulus and with the manually formed letter. The numerous repetitions provide adequate reinforcement and result in rapid learning. In the case of short "o" and "e" both are taught within a single week with no difficulty.

In the case of two letter digraphs such as "th" and "ch," the two letters are presented together as one manual movement. The emphasis is upon the beginning and ending positions of the movement. In this way, the children realize that they are to consider the two letters together and pronounce only one sound. Using the above procedure, "th" was taught in one lesson with perfect recall by all students on the following day.

After the new phonetic elements have been taught and needed old ones reviewed, the children should apply this knowledge to new words. Here the problems become ones of attention, sequencing, and blending. In order to reduce distraction, all printed material is removed. The teacher fingerspells the first letter in the new word. The children form the manual letter and vocalize the sound. If the sound is slow in coming, the teacher vocalizes it and the children repeat the fingerspelling and sound several times. Then the next "phoneme sign" is presented, returned, and vocalized. In this way new words are learned.

Total Communciation gives the teacher control of the letter being considered and the pace at which additional letters are presented. Active participation and attention is assured. Each child is constantly being checked even though she or he is a member of a group of two or three. After words have been fully presented and identified, the children are able to write them, even though they have never seen them in the text. Using the above lesson plan, it was not unusual to present ten related words in a single lesson and have them read with 100% accuracy the first time they were seen in list form in the book.

As the children in Ms. McKnight's class met these new words in stories in which there were many other words, they sometimes became confused. At this time, she used the manual alphabet as a guide. This help took several forms. Sometimes the child, particularly one who was inclined to reverse letters or words, would ask, "Is it a 'b' or a 'd'?" The teacher's response was to fingerspell the proper letter. Most often the student copied this and gave the sound. Then the child proceeded with no further help. In the event that the child could not recall the sound for the letter or letters the teacher fingerspelled, she gave the sound rather than the letter name. In this way, the letter stimulus was kept visual, and the appropriate sound paired with it.

If a child stopped reading because he or she did not know how to proceed, or started at the wrong end of a word, Ms. McKnight simply fingerspelled the first letter of the word giving difficulty and proceeded as she had for new words, that is, one letter at a time.

It often helps to remove the printed word from view enabling the teacher to control the progression and pace. When the word has been pronounced, the teacher points to it in the text, and the child pronounces it again and continues reading. Many times, particularly in the case of digraphs, the child will approach the word by sounding only the first letter. Usually all that is needed in this case is for the teacher to fingerspell the two letters. The child can then recognize that both are to be considered together. By guiding the child with fingerspelling and using verbal cues only when necessary, the teacher gives only the help which is absolutely essential. Thus, the children are encouraged to use all the skill at their command.

After the child is reading sentences with some fluency, the next skill introduced is the use of inflected endings, prefixes, and suffixes. Here again, sign language is helpful. In many signs each common prefix and suffix has its own sign (Charlip & Miller, 1974; Lake, 1976; Watson, 1964).

As indicated in Chapters 1 and 2, signs are not part of the manual alphabet, but the two are related in a way analogous to the relationship between shorthand and conventional writing. For example, the verb form "-ing" is shown in Figure 6. As another example, past tense is signified by throwing the signing hand back over the shoulder. By spelling a root word, then throwing the signing hand over the shoulder, not only is the "-ed" (past tense) signified but its grammatic function is shown (see Chapter 4: "Inflected Endings"). Apostrophes are shown by rotating the wrist, as illustrated in Chapter 4 ("Possessives").

By using these syntactical parts of sign language along with signs, a close relationship between the sign and the printed word is maintained.

ing verb form:
speak*ing*, sing*ing*, play*ing*, rain*ing*, danc*ing*, talk*ing*

Figure 6. The suffix "-ing" in sign.

Here, the child is able to use intuitive knowledge of English grammar to help with reading. If the child misses an inflected form, calling the word by its root form, the teacher gives the sign for the inflection, and the child can usually correct the error.

As the children became more familiar with the manual alphabet, they began using it to cue themselves. Many children find it easier to connect the visual letter first to its fingerspelled form and then to a verbal sound. (This is highly significant and an indicator of the value of Total Communication.) In fact, children often point to an unknown word with the nondominant hand and move through the word using the dominant hand for fingerspelling the letters. Without outside help, they often figure out an unknown word.

This tool was not consciously taught by Ms. McKnight, but was used by all three of her students with good to excellent results. In one case, the mother of a child told the teacher that her daughter had been reading with her cousin. The whole family was confused and somewhat stunned when she used her hand to figure out the words, but she amazed them with her success through this technique. As the year progressed, Ms. McKnight found it necessary to give permission to the children to "use their hands." Fingerspelling, like pointing, was used spontaneously in the beginning, then dropped when no longer needed. It was interesting that the children signed most carefully those parts of the words giving them greatest difficulty.

Closely related to the manual alphabet in teaching reading was the use of signs for whole words. These were added for nonphonetic sight words. For example, there was no point in manually spelling and sounding the word "come," because the sounds for those four letters have no meaning. On the other hand, the sign for "come" is similar to the gesture commonly used when motioning someone to approach. These signs, which are readily available in several books of sign language (listed in Appendix A) were quickly learned and useful in both reinforcing and in cueing the children. Here, again, the relationships between words became obvious. For instance, most words for male persons involve some gesture on the upper part of the face, and most of those for female persons involve a motion near the lower face. Thus, "boy," "man," and "grandfather" all use a similar location on the body, but different motions. These relationships were emphasized.

The three key children in Ms. McKnight's class made between 6 months and 12 months of reading progress in one school year, reading at 1.9, 1.9, and 2.2 on the WRAT Reading Test (Jastak, Bijou, & Jastak, 1963) at the end of the year. This increase was unusually high, particularly when compared to their previous lack of progress or to other children in previous years who were working in the same linguistic program but without Total Communication. All three children were reading in the beginning second grade book at the end of the year. They each achieved at least 90% accuracy on the last vocabulary test of this text. The original three each made a year's progress the second year of the study as well.

In addition to the techniques Ms. McKnight carefully developed, several other suggestions have been offered by classroom teachers using Total Communication. These are presented as vignettes below.

Signs were employed in teaching basic sight words (Dolch Word List) to three visual learners. Each student had a word box. Five new words were given each week. Five minutes were spent on the words daily. The teacher introduced the word with the sign. The students learned the words rapidly. Then once a word was learned, the children dropped the signs. The manual alphabet was used to teach the long and short sounds.

One little girl who was hyperactive, learning disabled and mildly hearing impaired used signs to help her reading skills. The teacher would sit in front of her and listen to her read. When she came to a word she was unsure of, the teacher would begin to sign the word. The little girl never taking her eyes off the page, would see the teacher sign with peripheral vision and immediately say the correct word. This technique of cueing a child on a word by using a sign will allow the child to never take his eyes off the page when he comes to a word he doesn't know. We have all taught children who look up at the teacher, lose their places, and then become frustrated when they approach a word they don't know. Many times we try to give the initial sound of the word—to no avail. Using the sign for the word seems to have solved this problem in reading instruction.

We have found sign (language) useful outside of teaching reading and spelling, particularly in the lunchroom where it is noisy. In two schools at least, older children have asked for information about sign as a result of seeing it used in the lunchroom and halls, or in contact with younger brothers or sisters who were using it in connection with reading or spelling. No stigma is attached to using the sign language. It is considered something that even "smart" kids want to know about. This is in sharp contrast to some of the kinesthetic alphabets, sandpaper and wooden letters that we have been using with our slow children. Hence, there is not the social resistance to using it. In fact, one first grade teacher was able to use her slower children to teach her more gifted ones the manual alphabet. This was a boost for the slower children.

AUTISM AND PSYCHOLOGICAL DISTURBANCE

The instructional model developed by Creedon (1973; Offir, 1976) for autistic children and others who are psychotically withdrawn starts with each child being seen individually for one to three 1-hour sessions a week. Then half-day classes are established for the children. These involve supervised group work (two to nine children in a group) and individual 15-to-20-minute sessions, all using signs with speech. Signs were emphasized. Fingerspelling was a minimal factor, especially in the beginning. In the afternoon recreational activities, such as skating and trips, were conducted.

The overall approach was behavioral with an emphasis on positive reinforcement. Initial rewards were food, tokens, and activities. Social remarks have become increasingly important with progress in the children's communication.

All of the 21 children who participated have progressed to using signs for immediate needs and for feelings. At the beginning all were functioning at the severely retarded level. In early stages they were echopraxic (the sign language equivalent of echolalic speech). Some would repeat a question, then add the answer. This is still done by some with new questions, just as all people commonly repeat a difficult question sometimes in order to clarify their thinking. There is also communication in sign between students, not just teacher to student. Simple sentences are now generated, but the progression was first individual signs, then two-word combinations and finally phrases and sentences. Some students use signs as an inner control of behavior, for example, "Stevie, don't!" or "Stevie, no!"

Along with signs for needs and feeling, those for colors, animals, clothing, body parts, proper names, and pronouns were taught early. Now, those who have been in the program 1 or 2 years are using 101 to 307 words. This vocabulary and the simple sentences used represent highly significant progress for autistic and for psychotically withdrawn children. Along with signing, some of the children are beginning to say the words. This behavior is intensely rewarded, but not demanded until the child has already fully mastered the word or sentence orally.

Behaviorally, it was noted that with Total Communication there was an increase in social activity, much less self-stimulation, and higher level play and use of objects. Some attempts at organized play with classmates also occurred.

Bonvillian and Nelson (1976) in their work with an autistic child used many of the same general behavioral and pedagogicial procedures as Creedon (1973). Their teaching also involves the two major advantages (molding and inconicity) they believe that signs offer in contrast to speech.

It is suggested that instructional periods be 30 minutes, during which new signs are systematically introduced and those previously learned are reviewed. In teaching a sign, two basic approaches are followed. In one the child's hand is molded by the teacher into the position of the sign and then guided through the motion required by the signs. The second technique is imitation. Both are used for all signs. The sign and spoken word are paired when presented to the child. Once the child can produce a sign, he is asked to identify the object or picture of the object for which it stands. Initially any reasonable approximation of the sign is accepted and rewarded. As skill improves the criteria for an acceptable (rewardable) reproduction of the sign are raised.

When possible it is important to involve the family. Once they learn and use a few signs, they find out how much easier it can make their life with their child. When this happens, the entire situation for learning is greatly improved. Even more important, this beginning communication improves the basic psychological climate in the home.

Everyone who has tried Total Communication (or any other method) with autistic or severely withdrawn students emphasizes the importance of being certain to have the child's attention before beginning. Therefore, the teacher starts by saying and signing, "Look at me." Once eye contact is made, the child is reinforced and the sign presented. If the child does not respond, his or her hands are gently guided to the desired position. Then the procedure is repeated. Direct eye contact, which is threatening to some autistic children, is not absolutely mandatory. If the child will look at the shoulders or face, the signs can be picked up by peripheral vision.

Once the children know a few "labeling" signs, they are asked, "What do you want?" This eventually leads to one sign or two or three sign responses. Eventually, the responses reflect an internalizing of syntax. Some children will eventually correct errors in their parent's or classmate's signs.

One point made by Creadon (Offir, 1976) is that instruction must go beyond a one-to-one relationship with a therapist or teacher using behavioral modification. This is why she feels classroom and recreational settings must be involved also. "We don't want these kids talking for M & M's all their lives," Creadon says (Offir, 1976).

Creadon makes another important point, namely that the real goal with these children is communication, not just speech. Too often the mindless imitating of sounds is seen as the goal. Actually, this often has no more communicative significance than when a parrot squawks out rote repetitions.

GIFTED CHILDREN

With the gifted, Total Communication is used in essentially the same way as with regular children, except earlier in their lives (see Chapter 2). Parents should be encouraged to learn fingerspelling and then to fingerspell and sign key words as they read to their children at night. As indicated in Chapter 2, gifted children fully exposed to fingerspelling and sign language before entering school are often able to read at an early age. In later years the complexity and uniqueness of American Sign Language offers gifted scholars a rich new field of study.

ADULT BASIC EDUCATION

The illiterate adult who has made the decision to learn to read through an adult basic education program faces a unique problem that Total Communication can help solve. Quite often, the decision to enroll is a difficult one. It is embarassing for an adult to admit his or her inability to read and write. For this reason, the adult basic education teacher must be very sensitive to the student's self-concept. This is not an easy task for a student learning primary grade skills from an adult frame of reference. Materials that are typically used in primary grades insult the adult learner and further erode self-concept.

Although some basic skills materials geared to adult interests do exist, there are not enough. Often limited budgets prevent adult basic education faculty from buying as many of the available materials as needed.

Total Communication, used as described throughout this book, is well suited to the adult learner since it carries no stigma and does not require purchase of expensive materials.

MENTALLY RETARDED

Sign language, and to some extent fingerspelling, has proven highly successful with mentally retarded persons (Fristoe & Lloyd, 1977; Mayberry, 1976). In the case of many trainable level individuals, it has made possible communication where none had previously existed. With higher functioning retarded persons, language skills, reading, attention span, motivation, speech, and imagination have been improved (Balick, Spiegel, & Green, 1976; Fristoe & Lloyd, 1977).

In addition to the general suggestions made concerning the use of Total Communication, there are some specific approaches that make the technique more effective with the retarded.

Use of Basic American Sign Language (ASL) Signs in an English Word Order

There are numerous artificial sign systems that have complex word endings and derivatives. However, these tend to make the task highly abstract and more difficult. By taking the signs exactly as they appear in any of the basic ASL dictionaries and putting these in regular English word order, maximum success is gained in improving language, reading, speech, and concept formation.

Fingerspelling

With trainable children, fingerspelling has little or no value and is not recommended. With educable level students, whether or not to use it or the extent to which it should be used is an individual decision based on the student's aptitude. In cases where the person can read or it is felt that the teaching of reading is a realistic goal, fingerspelling helps tremendously.

Sometimes in teaching the manual alphabet the students form the letters with their entire bodies at first. Once this has been mastered, they learn to form the letters on their hands. This is usually done using the whole word method, but the rule is not rigid (Figure 7).

Using the manual alphabet can be helpful in teaching phonics, for example, blends, digraphs, long and short vowels. The teacher should emphasize the blend, digraph, long or short vowel by using the manual letter or letters for it. (See section in this chapter on learning disabilities, pp. 15–18.) This skill helps with regular spelling, too.

Selection of Vocabulary

In beginning with manual communication, the new vocabulary should meet several criteria. First, functional words should be chosen. Second, the terms should be meaningful to the child and her or his needs. Third, iconic signs should be used, that is, signs that look like the concept for which they stand. Fourth, it is not advisable to introduce a whole lot of signs that are highly similar to each other in their hand formations, for instance, the signs for *pie* and *some*. Fifth, some children like touching and physical contact. For them, signs that can be taught by making them on the other person's body are excellent. Deaf preschoolers when first learning to sign often form the sign on their parent's body, usually the face (Figure 8).

Obviously, some signs meet all of the above criteria and others meet only a few. The important con-

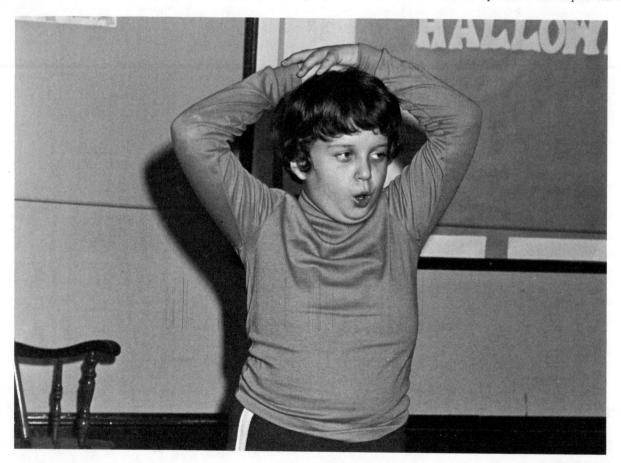

Figure 7. A retarded student forms the letter "O" with his body while saying the sound.

Figure 8. A deaf preschooler signs the word *mama* on her mother's face.

sideration is to keep these criteria in mind when selecting which signs to teach. The more of the criteria a sign meets, the greater the likelihood it will be learned.

Rate of Signing and Spelling

One of the major advantages of sign language and fingerspelling is that the stimulus can be sustained for as long as desired, that is, the rate of presentation can be fully controlled. This is not possible in oral communication because the meaning or "gestalt" of words and letters is distorted if sounds are sustained too long. This advantage of manual communication should be fully utilized with retarded students. The generalization is to go at a slow rate, but as one teaches an individual the optimal speed is worked out mutually.

Be Sure to Get Visual Attention First

Teachers are used to presenting lesson material to students who may be looking at their paper and writing, studying the chalkboard, or in other ways not watching. While this can be effective in oral communication, it is absolutely fatal with sign language and fingerspelling. When one is used to oral communication, it is easy to forget this basic rule. It is absolutely imperative that the student be visually attending the hands and face of the teacher when manual communication is taught.

Use of Voice and Manual Communication Together

In general, when a sign is made or a word fingerspelled, it should be spoken at the same time. This is the best application of both psychological conditioning principles and multisensory stimulation in that the learner simultaneously gets the stimulus visually (in both the sign and lip movement) and also receives it aurally. With certain cases where there is no receptive oral language, it may be best to begin with only the sign. However, there is insufficient data on this kind of problem to be certain about the best approach. The teacher's judgment on what is working best after trying both techniques is the most practical resolution of the problem. The following example illustrates one approach.

A speech therapist sought advice on how to get one of her students to communicate. The student's speech center in the brain was believed to be damaged and she could not talk. Previous advice by doctors and psychologists had recommended speech therapy. It had been unsuccessful. Kelly also was partially paralyzed on one side.

It was decided to try signs with her. The signs that she would have difficulty making because of her paralysis were modified. Her parents and the classroom teacher were cooperative. The speech therapist taught Kelly the signs. She used them to express herself. She did not really need them to understand what was being said to her because she got that aurally. The teacher used them in class and taught the other students how to sign. The parents used Total Communication at home. For the first time in her life, Kelly was able to express herself to her parents and classmates. Kelly is now trying to learn to talk with renewed interest.

Receptive or Expressive Language First?

In normal language development a child hears language for a year or more before starting to speak. Similarly, deaf infants of deaf parents see signs for a long time before using them expressively.

In the Total Communication Approach to language arts, initially the sign is first made by the teacher to the student. However, in most classrooms the student is asked to use the sign or to fingerspell the word very soon thereafter. This procedure is suggested as a general rule.

However, there is another dimension of the receptive/expressive issue. To the extent that it is feasible, the more often the student sees the teacher and classmates use Total Communication, the greater will be the amount of incidental learning.

Progression from Words to Phrases and Sentences

It is best to start with single words. Children and adults usually pick these up surprisingly quickly. However, there is then a tendency to try to move too fast (Fristoe & Lloyd, 1977). This can frustrate teacher and student alike. It is best to progress slowly, from single words to two and three word sentences or phrases, and on to fully connective language to ensure a high rate of success.

Steps in Teaching a Sign

There are three basic steps in teaching signs (Mayberry, 1976). One is imitation. For some learners all that is needed is the opportunity to copy the sign after the teacher makes it. Another is shaping, that is, actually putting the learner's hands and arms in the position of the sign. Finally, molding can be used

where the sign takes the shape of the object, for example, the sign for ball. Molding involves putting the student's hands around a ball, a positioning that forms the sign for ball.

Games Using Signs and Fingerspelling

Once basic manual communication is learned, games (see section on games in Chapter 4) can be played substituting manual for oral communication. This is a highly motivating fun period for most students.

The teacher should be pragmatic and willing to experiment in the application of the method. It is an adaptable approach of proven value with mentally retarded persons.

APHASIA AND COMMUNICATION DISORDERS

The primary use of Total Communication in the area of communication disorders has been with aphasics. In fact, not only have signs from American Sign Language been used, but some therapists have tried Native American signs (Skelly, Schinsky, Smith, Donaldson, & Griffin, 1975). However, the conventional signs of deaf people are strongly recommended because they are much more widely used in society today.

In beginning Total Communication with aphasics, signs should be selected that correspond to natural gestures, for example, "hush" (index finger to mouth), "yes/no" (head shake), "come here" (index finger motion). These basic signs are generally mastered fairly quickly. During this initial stage (and later) family and friends should be encouraged to use the signs to the extent possible.

Work should be done with the aphasics in both group and individual sessions and in incidental contacts. Receptive and expressive skills should be taught.

Next, signs involving basic needs and key subjects are presented. For the most part the signs selected are a matter of common sense, although a prepared list is available (Skelly et al., 1975). When possible, iconic signs should be introduced first. Also, teaching signs that are similar to each other can lead to confusion.

One technique of particular value in teaching expressive signing is videotaping. This nonthreatening approach enables the students or patients to correct their own errors. There are also films and books available (see Appendix A) that allow aphasic persons to work on their signing independently. Using mirrors has not proven satisfactory, perhaps because of the problem of the reversed mirror image.

In general, when lessons are presented, the instructor gives the sign manually and says the word for which it stands. The aphasic individual copies the sign and the mouth movement. Then, depending on the individual's ability, he or she is asked to vocalize the word. This work is often done in groups with responses made in unison.

With this approach even the most severely aphasic patients can generally master 50 or more signs in 2 months (Skelly et al., 1975). Some will be using 200 words and short sentences and phrases.

Because most aphasics retain an intact neuro-motor system for producing signs (Brain, 1965), they have been used more than the manual alphabet. Signs, especially iconic ones, seem to be bilaterally located in the brain in contrast to speech, which is a unilateral function (Battison & Markowicz, 1974). This obviously makes them especially helpful for aphasics. In fact, many aphasics unfamiliar with sign language actively gesture when trying to speak.

Signing and speech are essentially separate language functions (Battison, 1973). Fingerspelling, however, is a more direct representation of oral language. Thus, it is more severely impaired in aphasia than signing and gesturing. This would suggest that fingerspelling might not be of value with many aphasics, although isolated efforts give some suggestion that it has potential in certain patients (Battison, 1973; Battison & Markowicz, 1974).

Ironically, although actual efforts at using sign language with aphasics have proven successful (Balick, Spiegel, & Greene, 1976; Chen, 1971; Kadish, 1978; Skelly et al., 1975; Vernon, Coley, & DuBois, in press), some theoreticians have suggested that it will not work (Duffy, Duffy, & Pearson, 1975; Hamanaka & Ohashi, 1973/1974). Their position is based on test results, not on clinical findings.

Most other efforts to use Total Communication with speech and language disorders have involved communication disorders of psychological etiology, similar to autism or severe withdrawal (see "Autism and Psychological Disturbance" in this chapter). However, there may well be potential for its use with many types of speech problems. For example, when employed with deaf children, it seems to relieve some of the tension and trauma of the speech process, thus encouraging a more relaxed positive attitude and better oral skills (Vernon & Koh, 1970, 1971).

A similar application might be made with stutterers. If significant others (family, teacher, or therapist) learned fingerspelling and/or sign language, the stutterer would "have a way out" when caught in the embarrassment and humiliation of stuttering or "freezing" over a given word. Fingerspelling or signing the word would lessen the trauma of speech and the stutterer, freed from such anxiety, might do much better.

BLIND AND PARTIALLY SIGHTED CHILDREN

There has been only one known effort to use Total Communication with visually impaired children. It involved a special class with students ages 12 through 21, grade levels four through twelve, and IQ's of 68-110. The technique was applied in teaching reading and spelling (Figure 9).

Initially, the class was given the Dolch Word List. They were then grouped on the basis of their scores. Words were taught in the order in which they appeared in the SRA Reading Lab Program. Fingerspelling was introduced "phonetically," meaning that individual letters were not identified. Whole words or sounds were spelled as units. If a student forgot how to make a particular manual letter, the teacher would ask "What is the word?" Then the word would be spelled as it was said.

Signs were used only when words were too long to fingerspell. For example, Ilene could not spell "synagogue." Instead of persevering in an effort to teach the concept through fingerspelling, the sign for the word was given. After being shown the sign once, she was able to remember the word when she saw it in sight-saving print. In fact, the moment Ilene saw the word, she would make the sign and then say it to herself.

The same general approach was used with spelling, that is, the teacher would introduce the words by fingerspelling them. For the blind children, this was done by fingerspelling into their hands. With partially sighted students it was done visually, but close enough to assure perception of the hand positions.

Weekly tests were given. Sometimes, the teacher would spell the words. The students' task was to identify them. At other times, the teacher would say the word, which the students would then fingerspell. Reading tests were done in a similar way. Once students learned to read and/or spell their words, they dropped the signs and fingerspelling, which was appropriate.

It was found that fingerspelling helped reduce reversals that grow from the use of braille, for example "r" and "w." The manual letters are more distinctly different. Thus, it is important that fingerspelling be taught when braille is first learned. This procedure reduces reversals as a cause of reading failure from the beginning.

A final value of the method with blind children relates to "blindisms." It is common for some blind children when listening to a reading or spelling lesson

Figure 9. Two visually impaired students from the West Virginia School for the Blind work with large print and braille books. They are using fingerspelling to figure out unknown words.

to punch their eyes or rock. When the children were involved in fingerspelling or signing words, these habits were greatly reduced.

DEAF AND HEARING-IMPAIRED CHILDREN

Prelingually deafened[1] children face a fundamentally different process from that of hearing children when learning to read. For the hearing child, reading is essentially a matter of associating a printed symbol with an auditory one with which he or she is already familiar.

By contrast, the deaf child when learning to read is being asked to learn a new language as well as to master the printed symbols or words for this language simultaneously. If taught without Total Communication, the student is expected to accomplish this very abstract, difficult feat under conditions far more trying than many people fully realize. These conditions are

analagous to a hypothetical situation in which a student would be separated from a teacher by a sound-proof glass panel and required to learn a foreign language. In teaching, neither the instructor nor pupil would be permitted to use English as a frame of reference in any way. This situation illustrates the immense difficulties to be overcome by the deaf child in learning to read.

The situation of the average hearing child can be used to further illustrate just how much is being asked of the deaf child. The average child enters school with a vocabulary of about 5,000 to 25,000 words. Roughly speaking, the first 3 years are spent learning the printed form of these words already known. In addition to this relatively large vocabulary, the hearing student also starts school with a working knowledge of the syntax and idiom of the language, which has been developed through hearing. As a hearing child progresses she or he is required to master comparatively few new words through reading alone, but instead picks them up by oral communication supplemented by seeing them in print.

---

[1]A deaf child is defined as one whose hearing loss is of such severity that speech sounds cannot be understood.

This situation can be contrasted with the deaf child's. Instead of starting with 5,000 to 25,000 words and a working knowledge of how to join them together, the deaf child first learning to read often has no vocabulary or command of grammar. In order to read he or she must not only learn the printed words, but must also master the art of joining them together in an extremely abstract and complex manner which we know as the English language.

Looking at the situation of an intelligent, mature college student further illustrates the tremendous nature of this challenge. In 1 year of a foreign language she or he learns or is exposed to approximately 600 to 1,000 words plus the syntax of the new language. This is made simpler for the collegian because English is available as a point of departure and language principles and words that are similar in both languages can be transferred. Even if the young deaf child were able to equal mastery of 600 to 1,000 words a year, it would take at least 5 years to catch up with the hearing children with minimum vocabularies who were entering the first grade. That is to say, if she or he learned 600 to 1,000 words annually it would take this long to have the 5,000 to 6,000 word vocabulary of the average first grader. The average hearing child after 3 years in school can read most words that he or she can use in oral communication. The deaf child, and often the deaf adult, goes through life without knowing the written equivalent of many of the words and concepts they use in sign language every day. This of course, greatly complicates reading and is a source of vocational and social hardship to the deaf.

In view of the severe and unique reading/language problem faced by the deaf child, it is essential that Total Communication be started as early as possible, preferably by parents at the time the child is first discovered to be deaf. It must then be used continuously in all communication when the child is present. Only this way can the basic English language syntax and vocabulary be mastered. If this kind of Total Communication is provided, the deaf child's task in learning to read is very similar to that of the hearing child. Essentially, all she or he has to do is learn the print equivalent of the manual letters and signs already known.

When a deaf child has not had the benefit of extensive preschool Total Communication, the teacher has to introduce it. This means he or she must use Total Communication at all times possible. Often the only way to teach a sign is to identify it by a picture of the concept for which it stands.

The complexity of the education of a deaf child in the areas of reading and language are too profound to cover adequately in this chapter. However, the selected readings list at the end of this chapter gives the beginning information needed. The intent is simply to alert the teacher to the unique problem faced by the deaf child and the importance of early Total Communication in instruction.

Hearing-impaired[2] children face a problem similar to that of deaf children, yet one that is also different in some important ways. The hearing-impaired child can hear oral language well enough to develop at least a rudimentary syntax and vocabulary. However, sound is distorted sufficiently that such a child is hearing most words quite differently than they actually sound. Therefore, the standard phonetic rules and lessons are tremendously misleading in that the child does not hear what these rules indicate should be heard. For example, many hearing-impaired children miss consonant sounds, such as *s, t, sh, ch, z,* and *f.* Thus, there is direct conflict betwen the word as they hear it and the word as it is given in a phonetic reading lesson.

For this reason, the use of fingerspelling is of particular value with hearing-impaired children, when it is done simultaneously with speaking the word. It gives the children an understanding of the actual letters in the word as contrasted to the distorted sounds they hear, which are usually in conflict with the phonetic rules in basal readers.

Unfortunately, very few teachers will be able to fingerspell at a conversational speed, although this would be ideal for the hearing-impaired child in a reading class. However, a heavy emphasis on the procedures in the previous chapters will be of tremendous value to hearing-impaired children.

The role played by signs and fingerspelling is to ensure that the child perceived all of the words in sentences given to her or him. Only by perceiving all words can the child develop the normal syntactical patterns and vocabulary basic to reading.

SELECTED READINGS ON THE USE OF MANUAL COMMUNICATION WITH DEAF AND HEARING-IMPAIRED CHILDREN

Adler, E. A. Reading out loud in the language of signs. *American Annals of the Deaf,* 1964, *109,* 364-366.
Alterman, A. I. Language and the education of children with early profound deafness. *American Annals of the Deaf,* 1970, *115,* 514-521.

---

[2]The term *hearing-impaired* refers to a hearing loss in which the child can hear enough of what is said under ideal, quiet one-to-one communication to understand connected speech (with a hearing aid). Such children do not hear all sounds. When hearing-impaired children are in a situation where there are background noises, such as a classroom, they often understand little or none of what is said.

Bornstein, H. A description of some current sign systems designed to represent English. *American Annals of the Deaf,* 1973, *118,* 454-463.

Hoemann, H. W. Communicating with Deaf People: A Resource Manual for Teachers and Students of American Sign Language. Baltimore: University Park Press, 1978.

Hofsteater, H. T. 1959. *An Experiment in Pre-School Education.* Washington: Gallaudet College Press. Bulletin 3, Vol. 8.

Kenny, V. A better way to teach deaf children. *Harper's Magazine,* 1962, 61-65.

Scouten, E. L. The prelingually deaf child and his oral education in new perspective. *American Annals of the Deaf,* 1969, *114,* 770-776.

Wilbur, R. B *American Sign Language and Sign Language Systems.* Baltimore: University Park Press, 1979, pp. 229-258.

CHAPTER 4
TOTAL COMMUNICATION LESSONS, LEARNING CENTERS, AND OTHER ACTIVITIES

The preceding pages have explained in general terms the what, why, and when of the Total Communication Approach. This chapter gets down to specifics. It details the "how to" and gives ready-to-use plans for lessons, learning center activities, and games.

All teachers can effectively use the Total Communication Approach with no more preparation than reading this book. The manual alphabet and signs needed for most of the lessons and activities are shown on the page with the plan for the activities. A book of signs such as the *Signed English Dictionary for Preschool and Elementary Children* (listed under Appendix A) is helpful but not required.

A few basic guidelines relative to using fingerspelling and signs will facilitate initial experiences.

1. The hand and arm should be comfortable when fingerspelling or signing. Proper position for fingerspelling is with the elbow near the waist and the hand about 6 inches to the side of the chin.
2. Signs and letters should be made toward the class. That is, the palm generally faces the reader when fingerspelling.
3. The teacher should aim for clear, slow signs. With time will come a smoothness and a rhythm, but the signs should always be made slowly in this Total

Communication Approach, for quickly made ones are difficult to "read."

Lessons are provided in this chapter to serve as a springboard to help the teacher start immediately with the Total Communication Approach in the easiest, most effective way. Some of the activities also have reproducible student sheets, found in the back of the book.

The lesson plans and other activities concern reading and other language arts lessons. Each lesson plan contains a level of difficulty, materials needed, objectives, the function of signs used, the letters and signs needed, and the procedure. Some may be used exactly as they are. Others may be revised to meet the style of the individual teacher. Often, the lesson given will demonstrate how the Total Communication Approach can be used to teach a particular letter, suffix, set of vocabulary words, or other specific concept but can also be adapted to teach other letters, affixes, words, or concepts pertinent to the class.

It is suggested that a teacher using this book first look at the lessons indicated as appropriate for the level (readiness, primary, intermediate, or advanced) she or he teaches. Teachers should also skim the rest of the lessons because the grade level designation is not rigid. Many lessons can serve a range of levels with minor revisions.

Some teachers will find that they would like to change a particular lesson to provide more or less stimulus or a harder or easier evaluation. The objectives have been written informally so that the teacher who knows the needs of his or her class can snip here and tuck there to tailor the lessons to fit the students.

The reader is encouraged to think of other ways to use the Total Communication Approach to facilitate and motivate language arts learning and generally enhance life in the classroom (also see suggestions in Chapter 5).

LESSON PLANS

Lesson 1/LISTENING SKILLS

LEVEL   Readiness

MATERIALS   None

OBJECTIVE   Given a familiar song, the student will be able to supply the missing parts.

FUNCTION OF TOTAL COMMUNICATION IN LESSON

Every pupil response, motivation

LETTERS AND SIGNS NEEDED

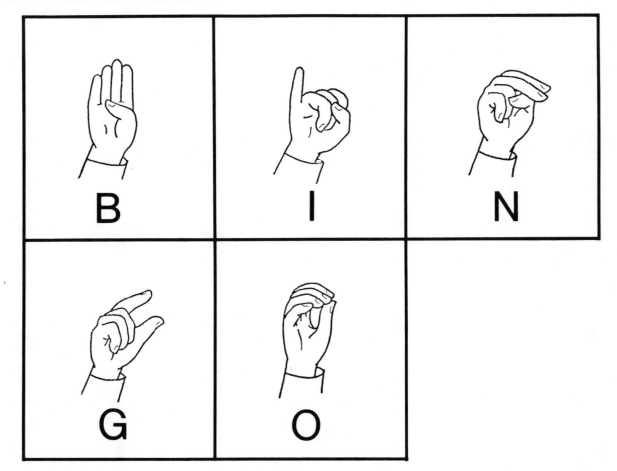

PROCEDURE   The teacher will introduce a familiar song such as "Bingo" in which the song is repeated over and over, leaving out an additional part each time. In this activity, rather than leaving out the part, the children will be asked to fingerspell the letter.

Bingo

There was a farmer had a dog.
Bingo was its name...Oh!
B-i-n-g-o
B-i-n-g-o
B-i-n-g-o
Bingo was its name...Oh!

There was a farmer had a dog.
Bingo was its name...Oh!
(B)-i-n-g-o
(B)-i-n-g-o
(B)-i-n-g-o
Bingo was its name...Oh!

There was a farmer had a dog.
Bingo was its name...Oh!
(B-I)-n-g-o
(B-I)-n-g-o
(B-I)-n-g-o
Bingo was its name...Oh!

The song should be sung a total of five times until all of the letters are manual alphabet letters (those shown in parentheses).

VARIATION   Other songs following this format can be used.

Lesson 2/LANGUAGE DEVELOPMENT

LEVEL   Readiness

MATERIALS   None

FUNCTION OF TOTAL COMMUNICATION IN LESSON
Illustrate concept

LETTERS AND SIGNS NEEDED

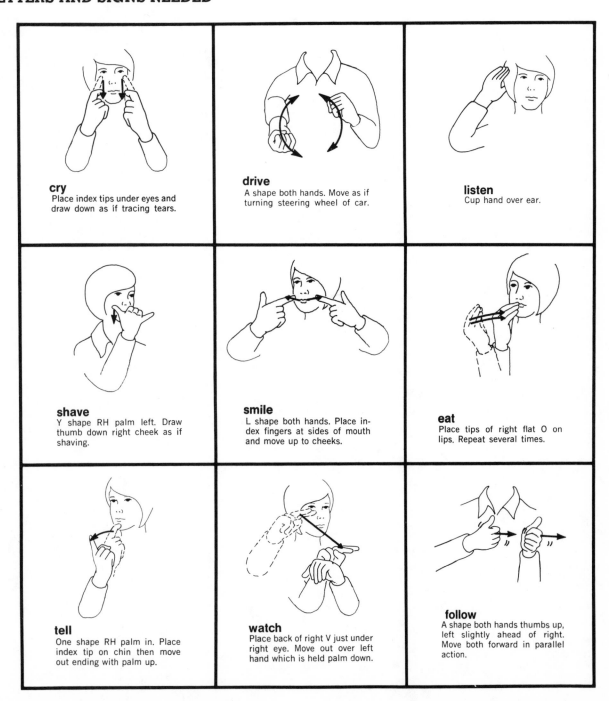

cry
Place index tips under eyes and draw down as if tracing tears.

drive
A shape both hands. Move as if turning steering wheel of car.

listen
Cup hand over ear.

shave
Y shape RH palm left. Draw thumb down right cheek as if shaving.

smile
L shape both hands. Place index fingers at sides of mouth and move up to cheeks.

eat
Place tips of right flat O on lips. Repeat several times.

tell
One shape RH palm in. Place index tip on chin then move out ending with palm up.

watch
Place back of right V just under right eye. Move out over left hand which is held palm down.

follow
A shape both hands thumbs up, left slightly ahead of right. Move both forward in parallel action.

PROCEDURE   The students should be told that people can sometimes tell what they mean without using words. The teacher should whisper an action word to each child in turn. Each student is to be given a few moments to pantomime the action. Other children can guess the action word. After several rounds have been played, the teacher can tell the class that some people say everything using actions like the ones they have been inventing. The teacher should briefly tell the children about sign language and then continue the game showing the sign for each action word after the student has had an opportunity to show her or his sign for the action.

VARIATION   For older students, adjectives can be used instead of action words.

Lesson 3/ALPHABET

LEVEL   Readiness

MATERIALS   None

OBJECTIVE   The student will use the sense of touch to reinforce the letter symbols of the alphabet.

FUNCTION OF TOTAL COMMUNICATION IN LESSON
Tactile/kinesthetic learning

LETTERS AND SIGNS NEEDED

PROCEDURE   As the kindergarten or first grade teacher introduces the letters of the alphabet a few at a time, he or she should also demonstrate the manual alphabet. The reason for showing the sign language letter whenever a letter is mentioned is to add the tactile-kinesthetic sense to the senses of seeing and hearing. Additionally, children can be shown sign language letters and asked to guess which letters they represent if they already know some letters. The fact that most of the sign language letters have a visual tie with their printed counterparts will help children whose learning is enhanced through the sense of touch.

Lesson 4/*AUDITORY DISCRIMINATION OF INITIAL CONSONANT SOUNDS*

LEVEL   Readiness/Primary

MATERIALS   Short story in which the target sound is used often. (This story can be improvised by the teacher.)

OBJECTIVE   Given a story told by the teacher, the student will show that he or she recognizes the target sound each time it occurs as the initial sound in a word.

FUNCTION OF TOTAL COMMUNICATION IN LESSON
Every pupil response

LETTERS AND SIGNS NEEDED

B	C	D	F	G
H	J	K	L	M
N	P	Q	R	S

PROCEDURE   The teacher will tell a short story slowly. The students will make the sign for the letter they are learning each time they hear it at the beginning of a word. At first, the teacher should stress those words that contain the target sound. As the children gain proficiency, the words containing the target sound can be made less obvious.

EVALUATION   The teacher will give a sentence orally which contains several words that have the target sound. The student will be asked to count the number of times she or he hears it at the beginning of words. The child may or may not be asked to use sign in the evaluation.

Lesson 5/INTRODUCTION OF CONSONANT OR SHORT VOWEL

LEVEL Readiness

MATERIALS Letter cards for the new letter and a few known ones if there are any. If none are known, two which are very different from one another should be taught.

OBJECTIVE Given a letter on a card, the child will say the sound it represents.

FUNCTION OF TOTAL COMMUNICATION IN LESSON
Tactile/kinesthetic learning

LETTERS AND SIGNS NEEDED
Alphabet (see Lesson 3)

PROCEDURE The teacher will show the new letter card, show the sign and say the sound. The child will be directed to show the sign and say the sound. This procedure should be repeated several times until the child can make the sign and sound comfortably.

    The teacher will show two letter cards including the one being taught. The child will choose the letter he or she is learning that day and make the sign and sound for it.

    The child will copy the letter and then make the sign and sound.

    Later in the day, the teacher can make the sign, have the child reflect the sign and say the sound.

VARIATION If other letter sounds are already known, those can be reviewed. The cards for these letters should be placed in front of the child. He or she will read the sounds and give the signs from left to right as the teacher points to each.

EVALUATION The card should be shown the following day and the student asked to give the sign and sound. If she or he can do this without prompting, the next letter can be introduced following the same procedure.

Lesson 6/INITIAL READING EXPERIENCE

LEVEL   Readiness

MATERIALS   Cards for letters and words (p, a, t, c, is, a)

OBJECTIVE   Given words which the child has practiced, he or she will be able to read a sentence made of those words.

FUNCTION OF TOTAL COMMUNICATION IN LESSON
Tactile/kinesthetic learning

LETTERS AND SIGNS NEEDED

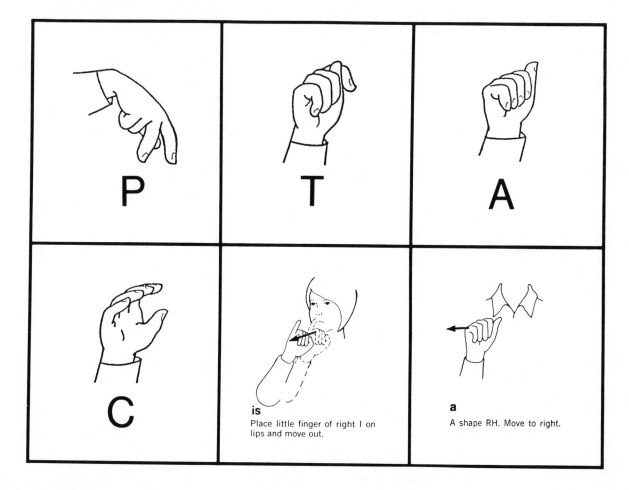

is
Place little finger of right I on lips and move out.

a
A shape RH. Move to right.

PROCEDURE   The sounds of the letters to be used should be reviewed. The teacher will place the letters in an order to spell a word, have the sounds read and signed in left to right order encouraging speed and blending until the child recognizes the word. If the child does not recognize it after a few tries, the teacher will read the word while signing the letters.

    Next, the teacher will show the same letters together on a word card and point out that they are the same and that they do represent the word. The child will be directed to look at the word, fingerspell it and blend the sounds.

    Word cards for "is" and the word "a" should be shown to the student. The teacher will tell the child the word and show the word sign.

The teacher will place the word cards in random order and have them read. The child can be prompted with the signs.

The teacher will place the cards in a sentence order. (For example, "Pat is a cat.") The child will be asked to read the sentence.

EVALUATION   Other sentences using the letters being practiced can be formed for the child to read.

Lesson 7/FINAL CONSONANTS

LEVEL   Primary

MATERIALS   None

OBJECTIVE   Given the beginning of a word, the student will supply final consonants to form words.

FUNCTION OF TOTAL COMMUNICATION IN LESSON
Every pupil response

LETTERS AND SIGNS NEEDED
(See Lesson 4)

PROCEDURE   The teacher will ask the students what is meant by a consonant. After reviewing the concept of consonants, the class should be told that they will be practicing consonants at the end of words. The teacher will write the beginning of a word such as "b i ____" on the board (or small slate or index card if working with a small group). He or she will direct the students to fingerspell letters that could complete the word on the board. The responses should be recorded and the class asked to read the words.

EVALUATION   The teacher can write two or three incomplete words on the board and ask the children to complete them on paper.

Lesson 8/RHYMING WORDS

LEVEL   Primary

MATERIALS   Classroom objects such as a book or map

OBJECTIVE   Given an object, the student will fingerspell and say the name of the object and a word which rhymes with the name of the object.

FUNCTION OF TOTAL COMMUNICATION IN LESSON
Illustrate concept

LETTERS AND SIGNS NEEDED
Alphabet (see Lesson 3)

PROCEDURE   The teacher will tell the class or group that they will be playing a rhyming game. The teacher will point to an object in the room, such as a book. A child should fingerspell and say the word for the object. The next student, or a child of the student's choice, is to finger-spell a rhyming word such as *look*. Play can continue until each has had a turn.

VARIATION   Teams of four children can be given a word and directions to think of as many rhyming words as they can. After 10 minutes of work time, a representative from each group can fingerspell and say the list.

EVALUATION   The teacher can lead the students into a discussion of why rhyming words "feel" so similar. If the children understand the concept, they will know that the pairs "feel" alike because they have the same ending letters.

Lesson 9/SIGHT WORDS

LEVEL   Primary

MATERIALS   Sight word flashcards or word bank cards

OBJECTIVE   The student will use the sense of touch to reinforce sight words.

FUNCTION OF TOTAL COMMUNICATION IN LESSON
Tactile/kinesthetic learning

LETTERS AND SIGNS NEEDED
Alphabet (see Lesson 3)

PROCEDURE   When sight words or word banks are practiced, the tactile/kinesthetic sense can be added to sight and sound by directing the child to fingerspell the word. The child should both sign and say the word she or he is seeing.

Lesson 10/CONSONANT BLENDS

LEVEL   Primary

MATERIALS   None

OBJECTIVE   Given consonant blends, the student will use fingerspelling to show the blend as a unit.

FUNCTION OF TOTAL COMMUNICATION IN LESSON
Illustrate concept

LETTERS AND SIGNS NEEDED
Alphabet (see Lesson 3)

PROCEDURE   The teacher will introduce blends as special letter combinations that "go together" to form one sound. She or he will choose one blend such as "sl." The blend should be demonstrated by making the sign language "s" and "l" very quickly. Everyone should practice until the blend can be made rapidly as it is being spelled aloud. The teacher will demonstrate fingerspelling a word with the blend such as *slat*. The group can spell other "sl" words being careful to do the blend quickly as one unit and then setting up a slow, deliberate pace for the rest of the word.

VARIATION   Children can use this activity with digraphs, diphthongs, and other letter combinations.

EVALUATION   Students can be asked to copy "sl" blend words from books they have. After the words have been copied, children can circle the blend with a crayon.

Lesson 11/BLENDING KNOWN SOUNDS INTO A WORD

LEVEL   Primary

MATERIALS   None

OBJECTIVE   Given a word which is regularly spelled but which is not immediately recognized by the child, the child will sign each letter in turn as he or she says the appropriate sounds.

FUNCTION OF TOTAL COMMUNICATION IN LESSON
Tactile/kinesthetic learning

LETTERS AND SIGNS NEEDED
Alphabet (see Lesson 3)

PROCEDURE   During directed silent reading, the children will be told to stop and point to any word they do not know and call the attention of the teacher. Under the direction of the teacher, the child will begin with the first phoneme of the word, sign it, and say its sound.

If the child is correct, the teacher will make no response and the child will go on to the next phoneme and then through the word.

If the child at any point gives no sign or an incorrect one, the teacher will give the correct sign. The child will imitate and proceed.

If the child's sign is correct, either because he or she knew the sign or because the teacher demonstrated it, but the sound is incorrect, the teacher should emphasize the sign by moving the signing three or four times within the child's field of vision. If the child still does not give the correct sound, the teacher will.

Once all of the sounds are reviewed in order, the teacher fingerspells the whole word, grouping the letters into phonemes. The child says the sounds as the teacher signs. The teacher by leading the fingerspelling thus controls the pacing and sequencing. With the teacher fingerspelling the word, the child by saying the sounds in order will generally recognize the word within three tries. If not, the teacher should tell the child the word. (Once learned by teacher and student, this procedure becomes automatic and rapid. As noted in Chapter 5, the student will often follow this sequence alone when reading independently after learning the steps.)

Lesson 12/VOWEL SOUNDS

LEVEL Primary

MATERIALS None

OBJECTIVE Given a word orally, the student will fingerspell the vowel sound which is heard in the word.

FUNCTION OF TOTAL COMMUNICATION IN LESSON
Every pupil response

LETTERS AND SIGNS NEEDED

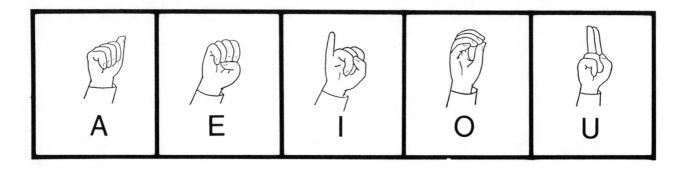

PROCEDURE The teacher will pronounce one syllable words. The members of the group will show the letter for the vowel sound heard.

VARIATION Again, the teacher can say one syllable words and direct the children to listen for vowel sounds. If the vowel heard is a long vowel, the students will make the vowel sign moving it back and forth in a straight line (indicative of a macron), and if the vowel is short, the students will make the sign for the vowel and move it back and forth in a curve to indicate a breve.

EVALUATION The teacher can say nonsense words such as *paff* and have the children indicate the vowel heard.

Lesson 13/INTRODUCTION OF A-T-E

LEVEL   Primary

MATERIALS   Word cards for *fat, hat, mat, fate, hate, mate, rate, gate*

OBJECTIVE   Given a sentence, the child will correctly read a new word ending in "ate."

FUNCTION OF TOTAL COMMUNICATION IN LESSON
Tactile/kinesthetic learning

LETTERS AND SIGNS NEEDED

PROCEDURE   The word card for *hat* should be shown and the students asked to fingerspell and read the word. The teacher should then show the card for *hate*. The students should be urged to discuss whether the words are the same and identify the difference. *Hate* should be fingerspelled and read.

The procedure will be repeated with *mat* and *mate*, and *fat* and *fate*. (If any of these words is new to the children, sentences can be used to illustrate the meaning.)

The teacher will line up words ending in "ate," and again have them fingerspelled and pronounced. It can be pointed out to the students that the words rhyme and feel alike.

The words *rate* and *gate* can be added to the list, fingerspelled, and read. The words should be used in sentences.

EVALUATION   Without telling the word, each child can be given a paper with the word "late" on it. They will be asked to illustrate a time this happened to them.

Lesson 14/INTRODUCTION OF SHORT O

LEVEL   Primary

MATERIALS   Word cards for *hat*, *pat*, *hot*, *pot*. Letter card for "o."

OBJECTIVE   Given a known three letter short vowel word, then replacing the vowel in that word with an "o," the student will read the word.

FUNCTION OF TOTAL COMMUNICATION IN LESSON
Tactile/kinesthetic learning

LETTERS AND SIGNS NEEDED

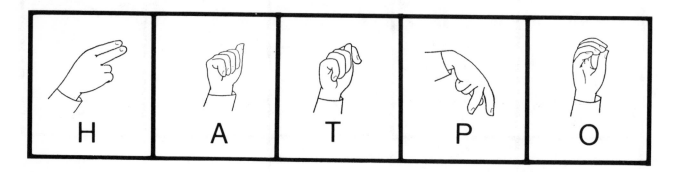

PROCEDURE   The class will use fingerspelling to review the known words such as *hat* and *pat*. The teacher will introduce the letter "o" making the hand position for the letter and saying the sound. It should be brought to the children's attention that the sign matches the mouth position for "o." The child will repeat the sound and sign.

The teacher will fingerspell hat, and then hot, and ask "What is the difference?"

The child will say the sounds and fingerspell *hot* with the teacher. The procedure should be repeated more quickly and the child asked, "What is the word?" The student will be directed to write the word on the board or paper and then fingerspell and read it.

The procedure will be repeated using *pat/pot*. The words can be read from the board or cards for further practice and used in sentences.

EVALUATION   The sentence, "The hat is in the pot." can be written on the chalkboard or a paper and the student asked to draw a picture to illustrate it.

Lesson 15/COMPOUND WORDS

LEVEL   Primary

MATERIALS   None

OBJECTIVE   Given the first half of a compound word in sign and orally by the teacher, the student will respond in sign with a reasonable second part for the compound.

FUNCTION OF TOTAL COMMUNICATION IN LESSON
Illustrate concept

LETTERS AND SIGNS NEEDED

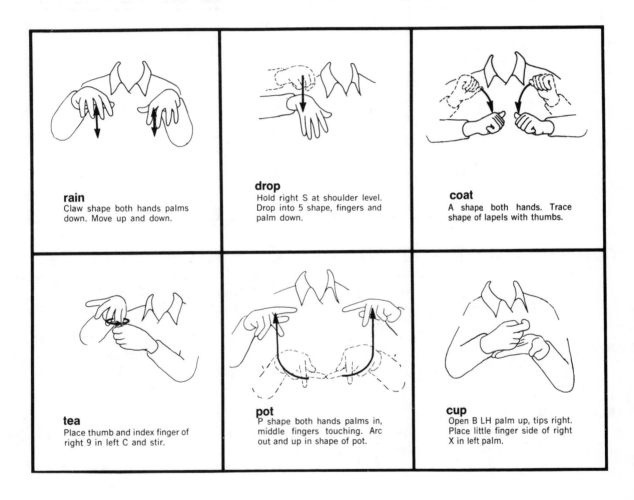

rain
Claw shape both hands palms down. Move up and down.

drop
Hold right S at shoulder level. Drop into 5 shape, fingers and palm down.

coat
A shape both hands. Trace shape of lapels with thumbs.

tea
Place thumb and index finger of right 9 in left C and stir.

pot
P shape both hands palms in, middle fingers touching. Arc out and up in shape of pot.

cup
Open B LH palm up, tips right. Place little finger side of right X in left palm.

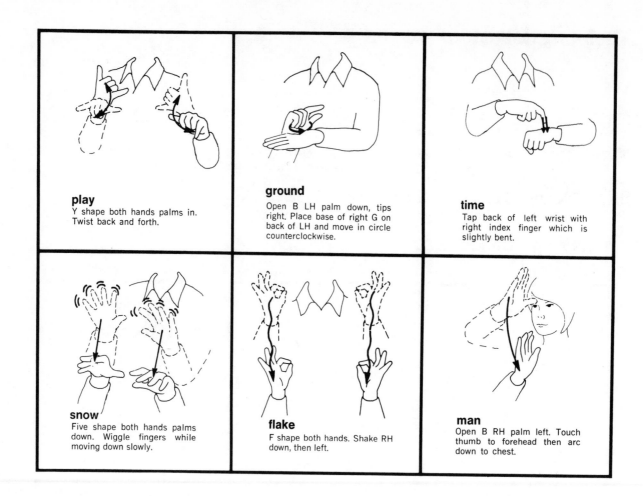

play
Y shape both hands palms in.
Twist back and forth.

ground
Open B LH palm down, tips
right. Place base of right G on
back of LH and move in circle
counterclockwise.

time
Tap back of left wrist with
right index finger which is
slightly bent.

snow
Five shape both hands palms
down. Wiggle fingers while
moving down slowly.

flake
F shape both hands. Shake RH
down, then left.

man
Open B RH palm left. Touch
thumb to forehead then arc
down to chest.

PROCEDURE The teacher should display and review the signs which will be useful in this lesson. He or she will then sign and say a first part, for example, *rain*. Students will respond with a sign for a reasonable second part, for instance, *drop*. The class will discuss the fact that compound words are made up of two different words signified by the two signs. Meanings of the words should be discussed.

VARIATION The children can be asked to invent signs for other compounds that could be made using the first part given. For instance, if a child wanted to form *rainspout*, he or she could make a motion like that in "I'm a little teapot," to indicate the answer.

EVALUATION During the day, the teacher will give the first part of a compound word in sign and orally. The child will respond as above. This activity can be done at odd moments to check understanding and reinforce learning.

Lesson 16/OPPOSITES

LEVEL   Primary

MATERIALS   None

OBJECTIVE   Given a word, the student will be able to state a word with opposite meaning.

FUNCTION OF TOTAL COMMUNICATION IN LESSON
Illustrate concept

LETTERS AND SIGNS NEEDED

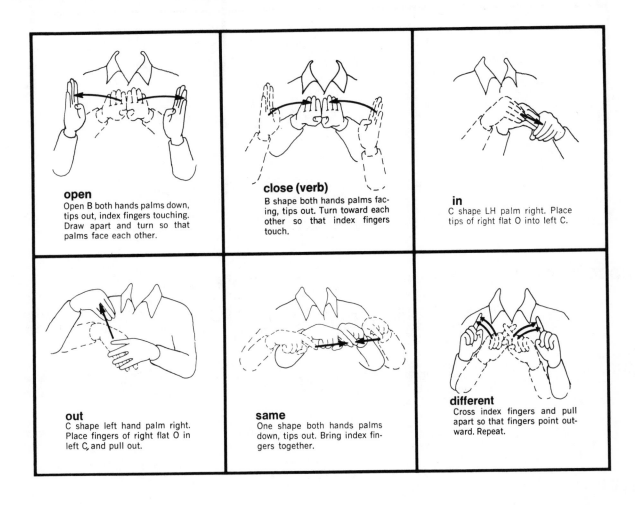

open
Open B both hands palms down, tips out, index fingers touching. Draw apart and turn so that palms face each other.

close (verb)
B shape both hands palms facing, tips out. Turn toward each other so that index fingers touch.

in
C shape LH palm right. Place tips of right flat O into left C.

out
C shape left hand palm right. Place fingers of right flat O in left C, and pull out.

same
One shape both hands palms down, tips out. Bring index fingers together.

different
Cross index fingers and pull apart so that fingers point outward. Repeat.

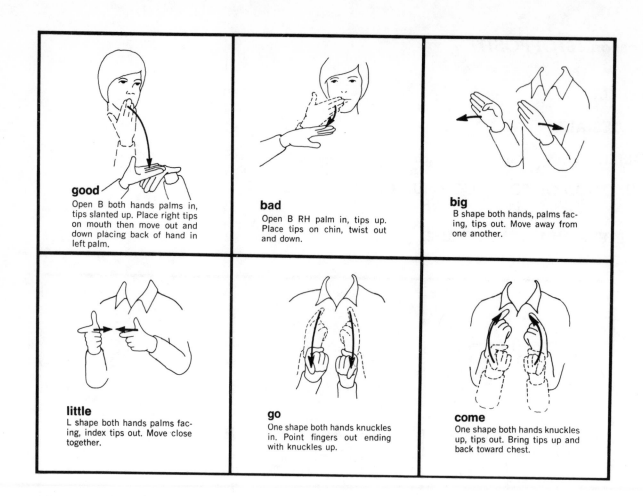

good
Open B both hands palms in, tips slanted up. Place right tips on mouth then move out and down placing back of hand in left palm.

bad
Open B RH palm in, tips up. Place tips on chin, twist out and down.

big
B shape both hands, palms facing, tips out. Move away from one another.

little
L shape both hands palms facing, index tips out. Move close together.

go
One shape both hands knuckles in. Point fingers out ending with knuckles up.

come
One shape both hands knuckles up, tips out. Bring tips up and back toward chest.

PROCEDURE
The teacher will discuss the meaning of the word *opposite*. The teacher will then illustrate by showing the signs for *open* and *close*. The children should be directed to imitate the two signs. The teacher can proceed by showing the sign for *in*. The students will try to guess the sign for *out*. Each of the pairs can be used, showing first the sign and then having the students guess the opposite and the sign for it.

EVALUATION
The teacher can prepare a sheet which contains words such as the ones used in the lesson. Each word should have a box beside it. In the box, students will draw an illustration to show the opposite of the written word.

Lesson 17/OPPOSITES AND SYNONYMS

LEVEL   Primary

MATERIALS   None

OBJECTIVE   Given two words orally, the child will be able to indicate the words as synonyms or opposites.

FUNCTION OF TOTAL COMMUNICATION IN LESSON
Illustrate concept

LETTERS AND SIGNS NEEDED
Standard signs in the class's vocabulary and any "home-made" signs invented by the class.

PROCEDURE   The teacher will ask the students to make a sign for little, then to make one for big. (The class may use standard sign language signs if they know them or make up signs.) He or she points out that the signs are different. This procedure should be repeated several times with other opposites.

After the children are familiar with opposites, the teacher can ask the children to make a sign for *little*, then one for *small*. She or he points out that the signs are the same or almost the same. This procedure is to be repeated a few times.

The teacher asks for a sign for *in* and one for *out*. Then he or she asks again, "Are the signs the same or different?" The teacher calls for signs for *tall* and *high* and repeats the question. Several sets of words are given, some synonyms and some opposites until the students are responding easily.

EVALUATION   On a numbered paper, the students make an "s" to indicate synonyms or "o" for opposites in response to sets of words the teacher reads.

Lesson 18/INFLECTED ENDING "-ing" AND REVIEW OF PAST TENSE

LEVEL   Primary

MATERIALS   Word cards for *walk*, *look*, *help*, *play*, *work*, *walking*, *looking*, *helping*, *playing*, *working*

OBJECTIVE   Given a dramatization of a regular verb, the student will make a statement describing the activity using the present participial form and demonstrating his or her recognition of the "-ing" in the word by making the "-ing" sign.

FUNCTION OF TOTAL COMMUNICATION IN LESSON
Motivation

LETTERS AND SIGNS NEEDED

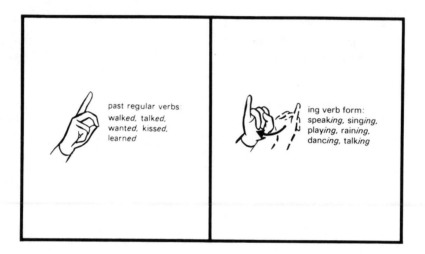

past regular verbs:
walk*ed*, talk*ed*, want*ed*, kiss*ed*, learn*ed*

ing verb form:
speak*ing*, sing*ing*, play*ing*, rain*ing*, danc*ing*, talk*ing*

PROCEDURE   The teacher will display the present tense forms of the words to be sure that they are known and discard any which are not. He or she will give the card with the word *walk* to a student and ask the child to do what the card says. The child will pantomime the word. If the student stops, he or she should be told to keep going. Then the teacher will ask "What is he (or she) doing?" The children will probably respond, "Walking." The teacher should model the answer in complete sentences by saying, "Yes, he (or she) is walking." While saying the ending on the word, the teacher will sign the "-ing."

The teacher will ask the child to stop and will ask, "What did he (or she) do?" A student should answer, "He (or she) walked," and the teacher will encourage the use of the sign for past tense. The procedure is to be repeated with each word.

The teacher will display the inflected cards and read each showing the sign for "-ing" each time it is said. The students will match each inflected word with its base word.

The teacher can give a base word to each child. Each, in turn, should demonstrate the word. When another student identifies what he or she is doing, the answering child will find the card that says the word for the action. All of the children will read this card and show the ending with the "-ing" sign.

EVALUATION   The teacher will whisper a regular verb to each student. The children will take turns demonstrating their words. The rest will guess what is being shown, using the "-ing" sign when stating each guess.

Lesson 19/POSSESSIVES

LEVEL   Primary

MATERIALS   A personal possession belonging to each child such as a hat or toy

OBJECTIVE   Given an article, the student will indicate in sign "'s" following the name to signify possession of that article.

FUNCTION OF TOTAL COMMUNICATION IN LESSON
Every pupil response

LETTERS AND SIGNS NEEDED
Name signs for each student in the group (to be invented by the class)

possessive:
cat's, dog's, pig's,
bear's, grandmother's

PROCEDURE   The children should seat themselves in a circle. Each will be given an article which belongs to another child in the group. One child will be asked to hold up the article which he or she has and ask, "Whose _____?" The others in the group will respond by signing the owner's name and "'s."

   The owner of the article then has a chance to hold up the article he or she has and repeat the procedure. Play continues until all the articles have been used.

EVALUATION   The teacher will hold up something known to belong to someone outside the class. Students will respond in sign with the person's initials (or name sign) followed by "'s."

Lesson 20/CONTRACTIONS

LEVEL   Primary

MATERIALS   None

OBJECTIVE   Having been told two words which can be contracted the child will sign both the two words and the contraction.

FUNCTION OF TOTAL COMMUNICATION IN LESSON
Illustrate concept

LETTERS AND SIGNS NEEDED

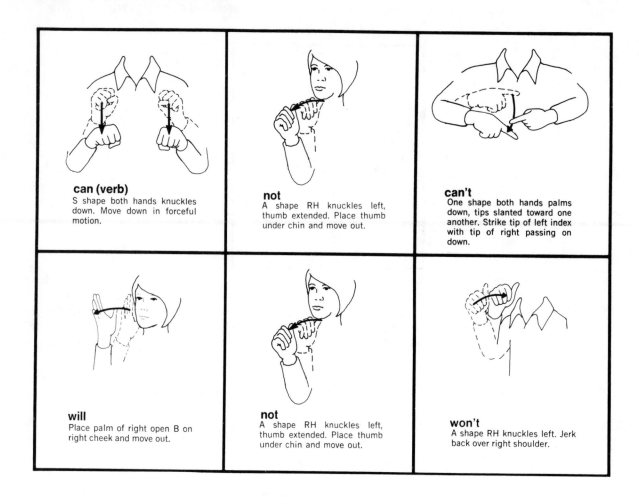

can (verb)
S shape both hands knuckles down. Move down in forceful motion.

not
A shape RH knuckles left, thumb extended. Place thumb under chin and move out.

can't
One shape both hands palms down, tips slanted toward one another. Strike tip of left index with tip of right passing on down.

will
Place palm of right open B on right cheek and move out.

not
A shape RH knuckles left, thumb extended. Place thumb under chin and move out.

won't
A shape RH knuckles left. Jerk back over right shoulder.

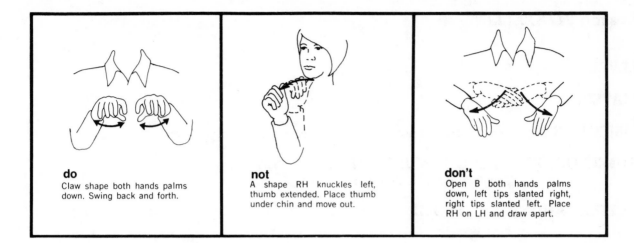

do
Claw shape both hands palms down. Swing back and forth.

not
A shape RH knuckles left, thumb extended. Place thumb under chin and move out.

don't
Open B both hands palms down, left tips slanted right, right tips slanted left. Place RH on LH and draw apart.

PROCEDURE The teacher will say the words *can* and *not*, at the same time he or she demonstrates the signs for these words. The students will imitate the signs. The signs will then be repeated in such a way as to emphasize that they are two distinct words with two separate signs.

The teacher will demonstrate *can't* making the movement as smooth as possible and ask, "Which is quicker?"

The children will sign first *can not* and then *can't*. The same procedure is to be followed for the other contractions until the children have made the generalization that a contraction is a shortened form.

EVALUATION The teacher will ask a child to sign and say both the two words and the contraction for a set of words studied in this lesson.

Lesson 21/SPELLING

LEVEL   Primary/Intermediate

MATERIALS   Spelling list

OBJECTIVE   The student will use fingerspelling to practice spelling words.

FUNCTION OF TOTAL COMMUNICATION IN LESSON
Tactile/kinesthetic learning

LETTERS AND SIGNS NEEDED
Alphabet (see Lesson 3)

PROCEDURE   The teacher will direct students to put their spelling lists on their desks. The children will be asked to work on each word in turn. They will fingerspell a word twice, looking at the list. They will then be asked to look away from the list to try to write the word. Finally, the students are to check the written word to see if it is correct. If so, the student may go on to repeat the procedure with the next word. If not, the procedure should be repeated with the word that was incorrect.

VARIATION   The teacher can fingerspell the words and the children can write them on their papers.

EVALUATION   A traditional spelling test can be given. Another method is to have students work in pairs. One child can dictate words from the list. The other can fingerspell and say the dictated words slowly.

Lesson 22/SPELLING

LEVEL   Primary/Intermediate

MATERIALS   Class spelling list

OBJECTIVE   Given a list of spelling words to be practiced, the student will use fingerspelling as part of a group activity involving both the giving and receiving of the words on the list.

FUNCTION OF TOTAL COMMUNICATION IN LESSON
Tactile/kinesthetic learning

LETTERS AND SIGNS NEEDED
Alphabet (see Lesson 3)

PROCEDURE   The teacher will write the spelling words on the board. Students will sit in a circle and watch as the teacher fingerspells one of the words slowly. The children should attempt to determine which word is being spelled. The child who is able to identify the word, finger-spell it, and say the letters is allowed to choose the next word to be fingerspelled for the group to identify.

EVALUATION   A traditional spelling test can be used to evaluate.

Lesson 23/SILENT LETTERS IN SPELLING

LEVEL   Primary/Intermediate

MATERIALS   List of spelling words including ones with silent letters

OBJECTIVE   Students will spell aloud the voiced letter and sign the silent letters.

FUNCTION OF TOTAL COMMUNICATION IN LESSON
Illustrate concept

LETTERS AND SIGNS NEEDED
Alphabet (see Lesson 3)

PROCEDURE   The teacher will ask the children to spell the words in unison. They are to say each letter that has a sound and sign each silent letter.

VARIATION   This method of spelling can also be used to give new interest to familiar games and activities commonly used to practice spelling.

EVALUATION   Each child can be given words to spell. He or she can be directed to write the words and underline the letters which have a sound.

Lesson 24/INITIAL CONSONANTS

LEVEL Primary/Intermediate

MATERIALS Polaroid camera, pictures of nouns representing the initial consonants to be studied (at least one per child)

OBJECTIVE Given a word, the student will indicate the initial consonant by inventing a handsign which employs the initial consonant.

FUNCTION OF TOTAL COMMUNICATION IN LESSON
Motivation

LETTERS AND SIGNS NEEDED
Signs to be invented by students

PROCEDURE The teacher will distribute noun cards. Each child will be responsible for inventing a sign for the noun on her or his card. The signs must be initialized, that is, the first letter of the word must be used in the sign. For example, for the word *snake* a sign language "s" wriggled like a snake could be used. As each student is ready, he or she can be taken into the hall and photographed signing the word.

The next day, all the words should be written on the board. Each student will be given his or her picture. One at a time, they will come up front and sign their words. The other children must guess the noun and tell its initial consonant.

VARIATION The invented signs can be compared to the formal signs found in a sign language dictionary. The photos and word cards can be used as the basis of a matching center.

EVALUATION Students can be asked to draw pictures for various noun words. The initial consonant must be incorporated into the picture.

Lesson 25/SUFFIXES (-s, -es)

LEVEL   Primary/Intermediate

MATERIALS   Word cards

OBJECTIVE   Given a word, the student will indicate whether -s or -es must be added to form the plural.

FUNCTION OF TOTAL COMMUNICATION IN LESSON
Every pupil response

LETTERS AND SIGNS NEEDED

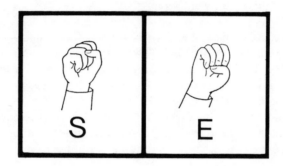

PROCEDURE   The teacher will explain that she or he will show the group words. If "es" must be added to make the word plural, the students should make the sign language "es." If only "s" is needed for a word, "s" should be shown.

VARIATION   The activity can be used with other suffixes.

EVALUATION   The children should be asked to search in the basal reader for three singular words to which "es" would have to be added to form the plural and three to which "s" would have to be added.

Lesson 26/FACT-FANTASY

LEVEL   Primary/Intermediate

MATERIALS   Basal reader

OBJECTIVE   After reading a story, students will use fingerspelling to indicate whether the events in the story are impossible or real.

FUNCTION OF TOTAL COMMUNICATION IN LESSON
Every pupil response

LETTERS AND SIGNS NEEDED

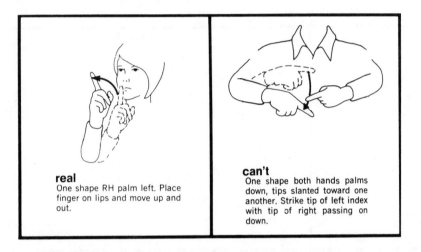

real
One shape RH palm left. Place finger on lips and move up and out.

can't
One shape both hands palms down, tips slanted toward one another. Strike tip of left index with tip of right passing on down.

PROCEDURE   This activity should be used at the completion of a basal reader or a section of one. The teacher will initiate a discussion of fact (real) versus fantasy (impossible). Children should be introduced to both signs. When there is general understanding of the difference, children in the group will be directed to turn to the beginning of the basal and review the first story. They will then be asked to vote on whether they think all of the events in the story could be real or whether some of them are impossible. The signs for *real* and *impossible* (or can't) will be used to indicate answers. The procedure will be repeated with several stories in the book.

EVALUATION   Class members can be asked to write two factual sentences about themselves and two fantasy sentences about themselves.

Lesson 27/READING COMPREHENSION

LEVEL   Intermediate

MATERIALS   Story

OBJECTIVE   Given a who, what, when, where, or why question about a story, the student will demonstrate comprehension by answering appropriately.

FUNCTION OF TOTAL COMMUNICATION IN LESSON
Motivation

LETTERS AND SIGNS NEEDED

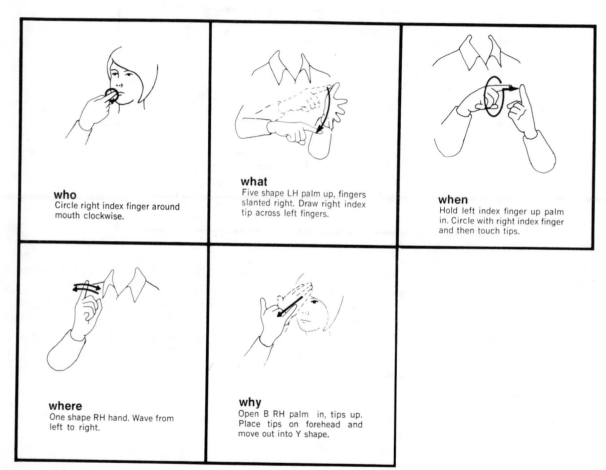

who
Circle right index finger around mouth clockwise.

what
Five shape LH palm up, fingers slanted right. Draw right index tip across left fingers.

when
Hold left index finger up palm in. Circle with right index finger and then touch tips.

where
One shape RH hand. Wave from left to right.

why
Open B RH palm in, tips up. Place tips on forehead and move out into Y shape.

PROCEDURE   This technique should be used after a basal reader story or story from another source has been shared by a group. The teacher will familiarize the group with the five signs. He or she will start the activity by making one of the signs to a group member. The student will answer the question relative to the story. For instance, if the teacher has made the sign for *where*, the student must tell where the story took place. The responding student will make one of the remaining signs to another classmate and so on. Once learned, this activity can be used as a quick comprehension check for any story heard or read.

EVALUATION   After doing the activity, students can be directed to write a one paragraph newspaper article which tells about the story events and includes the answer to the five questions.

Lesson 28/CONTEXT CLUES

LEVEL   Intermediate

MATERIALS   Sentences

OBJECTIVE   The student will use context clues to supply missing words in sentences.

FUNCTION OF TOTAL COMMUNICATION IN LESSON
Every pupil response

LETTERS AND SIGNS NEEDED
Any signs currently in the class's sign language vocabulary or "home-made" signs.

PROCEDURE   The teacher will tell the class that she or he will be reading sentences which have words missing from them. When the teacher comes to the missing words, the class members are to use the sense of the sentence to figure out what the words should be. When a student has an answer, he or she will make the sign for the word. For example, if the class knows the sign (or can invent a sign) for *hat*, the teacher could say, "Jill put a _____ on her head."

VARIATION   If the students know enough signs, the teacher may read a story from the basal or other book, leaving out strategic words. The students will make signs for the missing words.

Lesson 29/CHARACTER FEELINGS AND EMOTIONS

LEVEL   Intermediate

MATERIALS   Basal reader story

OBJECTIVE   Given a character and situation from a basal reader, the student will demonstrate comprehension by indicating how the character felt in that situation.

FUNCTION OF TOTAL COMMUNICATION IN LESSON
Every pupil response

LETTERS AND SIGNS NEEDED

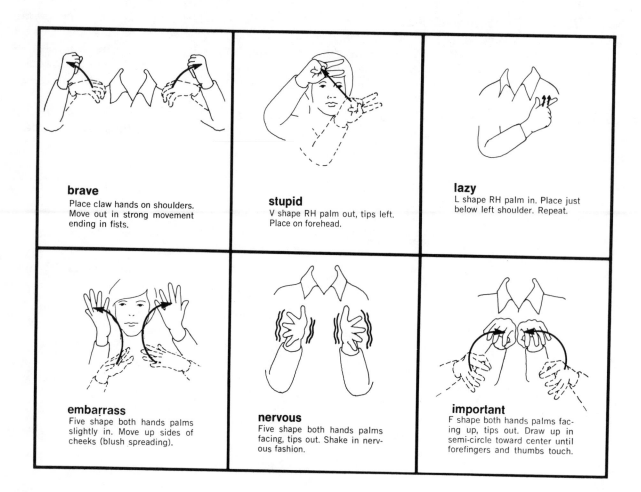

brave
Place claw hands on shoulders. Move out in strong movement ending in fists.

stupid
V shape RH palm out, tips left. Place on forehead.

lazy
L shape RH palm in. Place just below left shoulder. Repeat.

embarrass
Five shape both hands palms slightly in. Move up sides of cheeks (blush spreading).

nervous
Five shape both hands palms facing, tips out. Shake in nervous fashion.

important
F shape both hands palms facing up, tips out. Draw up in semi-circle toward center until forefingers and thumbs touch.

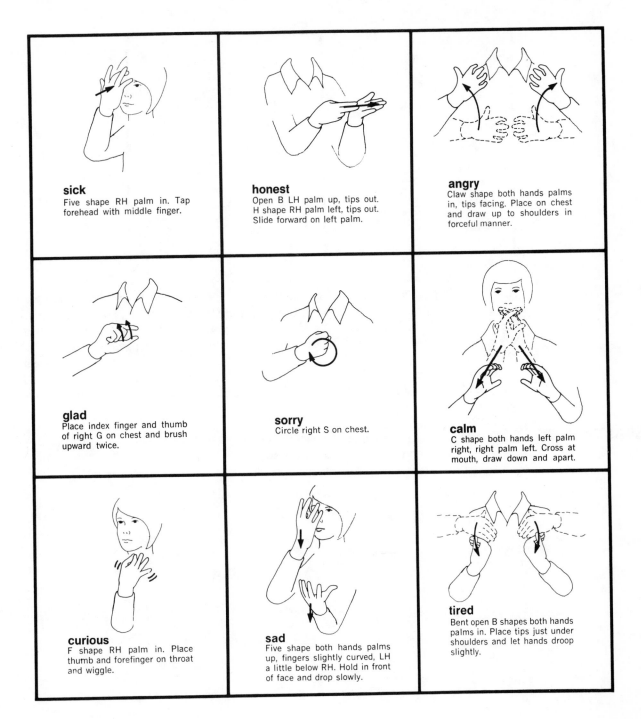

sick
Five shape RH palm in. Tap forehead with middle finger.

honest
Open B LH palm up, tips out. H shape RH palm left, tips out. Slide forward on left palm.

angry
Claw shape both hands palms in, tips facing. Place on chest and draw up to shoulders in forceful manner.

glad
Place index finger and thumb of right G on chest and brush upward twice.

sorry
Circle right S on chest.

calm
C shape both hands left palm right, right palm left. Cross at mouth, draw down and apart.

curious
F shape RH palm in. Place thumb and forefinger on throat and wiggle.

sad
Five shape both hands palms up, fingers slightly curved, LH a little below RH. Hold in front of face and drop slowly.

tired
Bent open B shapes both hands palms in. Place tips just under shoulders and let hands droop slightly.

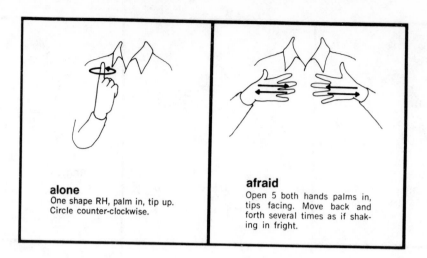

alone
One shape RH, palm in, tip up.
Circle counter-clockwise.

afraid
Open 5 both hands palms in,
tips facing. Move back and
forth several times as if shak-
ing in fright.

PROCEDURE

After the group has had a chance to read the story, the teacher can introduce this activity. The teacher or students will cite a character and situation from the story. (For example, if the class had read *Little Red Riding Hood*, the following could be used: Little Red Riding Hood when she saw the wolf.) Group members will be asked to make the sign that shows how the character felt at that point. Several children can be asked to share the reasons for their answers. Once introduced, this technique can be used briefly after any story. It is suggested that the signs and their meanings be displayed the first few times this activity is used.

EVALUATION

Students can be given a list of characters and asked to draw simple pictures to show how each felt at the beginning and end of the story.

Lesson 30/EXPRESSIVE ORAL READING

LEVEL   Intermediate

MATERIALS   Sentences on chalkboard, basal reader

OBJECTIVE   Given a sentence, the student will use voice and signing to repeat it expressively.

FUNCTION OF TOTAL COMMUNICATION IN LESSON
Illustrate concept

LETTERS AND SIGNS NEEDED

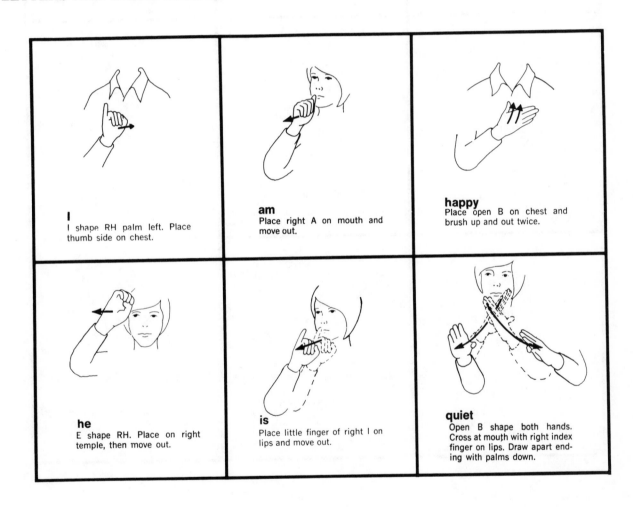

I
I shape RH palm left. Place thumb side on chest.

am
Place right A on mouth and move out.

happy
Place open B on chest and brush up and out twice.

he
E shape RH. Place on right temple, then move out.

is
Place little finger of right I on lips and move out.

quiet
Open B shape both hands. Cross at mouth with right index finger on lips. Draw apart ending with palms down.

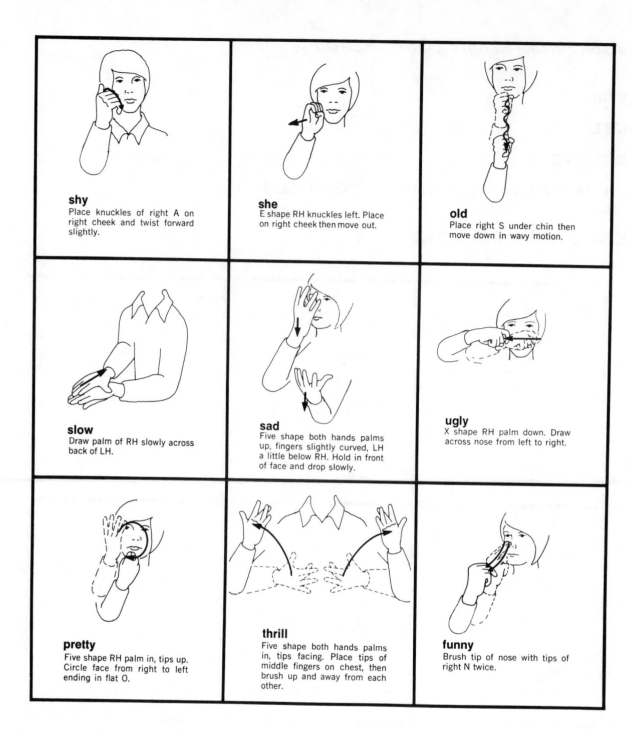

shy
Place knuckles of right A on right cheek and twist forward slightly.

she
E shape RH knuckles left. Place on right cheek then move out.

old
Place right S under chin then move down in wavy motion.

slow
Draw palm of RH slowly across back of LH.

sad
Five shape both hands palms up, fingers slightly curved, LH a little below RH. Hold in front of face and drop slowly.

ugly
X shape RH palm down. Draw across nose from left to right.

pretty
Five shape RH palm in, tips up. Circle face from right to left ending in flat O.

thrill
Five shape both hands palms in, tips facing. Place tips of middle fingers on chest, then brush up and away from each other.

funny
Brush tip of nose with tips of right N twice.

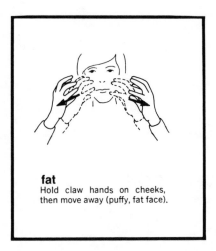

fat
Hold claw hands on cheeks,
then move away (puffy, fat face).

PROCEDURE

The sentences will be put on the board or chart paper before the lesson. In introducing the lesson, the teacher can explain that people who use sign language use their faces as well as their hands to talk. Facial expression for a deaf person can be compared to tone of voice in a hearing person. The teacher should show the signs for each of the sentences. The teacher's signs should be done in a dull, expressionless way. A student will be asked to repeat each signed sentence. The student, however, should be directed to show with her or his face what the signs mean. After everyone has had a chance to experiment with facial expression, the activity can be repeated with children both signing and saying the sentences. Children should be encouraged to add voice expression to the facial expression. Finally, attention should be switched to the current basal reader story. Students should be asked to apply voice and facial expression to story passages by having a turn to read part of the story in an animated way.

EVALUATION

A learning center with cassette tape recorder and a paragraph can be set up. Children can be asked to practice reading the paragraph and then tape themselves reading it. After many students have visited the center, the teacher can listen to the tape and diagnose progress.

Lesson 31 / FACT-OPINION

LEVEL   Intermediate

MATERIALS   None

OBJECTIVE   Given a sentence made up by a student, the student will indicate whether it is a statement of fact or opinion.

FUNCTION OF TOTAL COMMUNICATION IN LESSON
Every pupil response

LETTERS AND SIGNS NEEDED

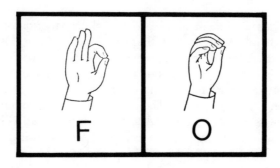

PROCEDURE   The teacher should initiate a discussion of the difference between fact and opinion. Examples should be provided. Each child in the group will then be directed to make up a sentence. As each student takes a turn saying her or his sentence, the other members will make an "f" if the sentence is a statement of fact or an "o" if it is a statement of opinion.

EVALUATION   A written sheet of statements can be prepared for the students. Either the teacher can read the sentences aloud or students can read them silently. The children will write "f" by factual sentences and "o" by opinions.

Lesson 32/SYLLABLES

LEVEL Intermediate

MATERIALS Word cards

OBJECTIVE Given a word on a card, the student will use fingerspelling to indicate the syllables in the word.

FUNCTION OF TOTAL COMMUNICATION IN LESSON
Illustrate concept

LETTERS AND SIGNS NEEDED
Alphabet (see Lesson 3)

PROCEDURE Each child will be given a word card. The student's task will be to practice fingerspelling the word in syllables. For example, a child who had the word *basketball* on the card would fingerspell, "bas-(pause)ket-(pause)ball." After practice, each child will be asked to spell her or his word for the group using fingerspelling. The group members should say the syllables aloud as they are spelled.

EVALUATION Strips of scrap paper can be distributed. Students will be directed to copy a spelling word on each strip and then fold the paper to show syllable divisions.

Lesson 33/PARTS OF SPEECH

LEVEL   Intermediate

MATERIALS   None

OBJECTIVE   Given a word in a sentence, the student will indicate whether the word is used as a noun, verb, or adjective.

FUNCTION OF TOTAL COMMUNICATION IN LESSON
Every pupil response

LETTERS AND SIGNS NEEDED

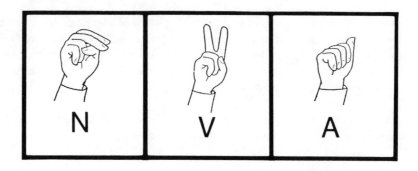

PROCEDURE   The teacher should divide the class or group into three sections: noun, verb, and adjective. The teacher will read sentences to the class, strongly emphasizing one word. (These can be sentences written and submitted by the children.) If that word is an adjective, the adjective section of the group should make the sign language letter "a." If it is a noun, the letter "n" will be shown by the noun section. If the word used is a verb, the verb students will show a "v."

EVALUATION   The rules of the activity can be changed so that when the teacher reads the sentence, all students are to make the letter to show the part of speech of the emphasized word.

Lesson 34/HOMOPHONES

LEVEL   Intermediate

MATERIALS   None

OBJECTIVE   Given an oral sentence containing a homophone, the student will indicate the correct form of the homophone by making the sign for it.

FUNCTION OF TOTAL COMMUNICATION IN LESSON
Illustrate concept

LETTERS AND SIGNS NEEDED

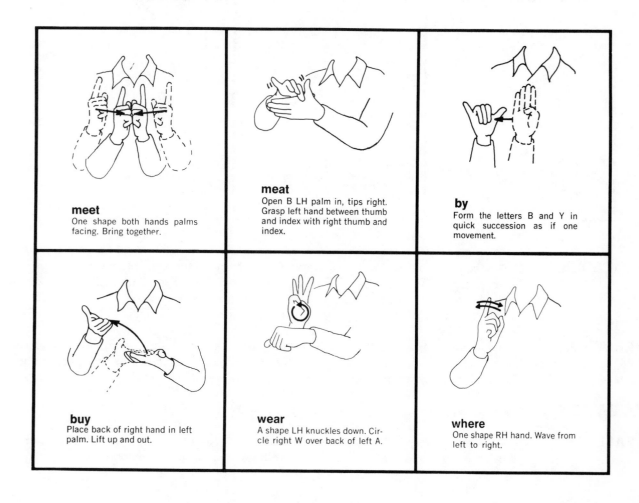

meet
One shape both hands palms facing. Bring together.

meat
Open B LH palm in, tips right. Grasp left hand between thumb and index with right thumb and index.

by
Form the letters B and Y in quick succession as if one movement.

buy
Place back of right hand in left palm. Lift up and out.

wear
A shape LH knuckles down. Circle right W over back of left A.

where
One shape RH hand. Wave from left to right.

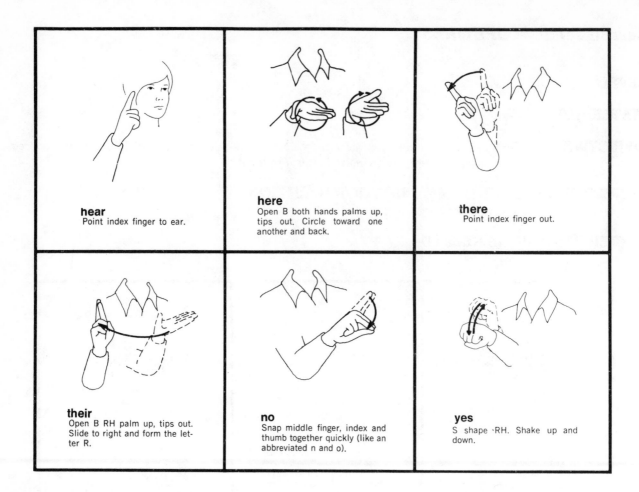

hear
Point index finger to ear.

here
Open B both hands palms up, tips out. Circle toward one another and back.

there
Point index finger out.

their
Open B RH palm up, tips out. Slide to right and form the letter R.

no
Snap middle finger, index and thumb together quickly (like an abbreviated n and o).

yes
S shape ·RH. Shake up and down.

PROCEDURE   The teacher or a student will give a sentence with one of the homophones being studied. For example, "*There* goes Jim." A student will be chosen to sign and say the form of the homophone which is appropriate to the sentence. (The signs should be reviewed and displayed before the lesson.)

VARIATION   The student can be given the option of bluffing and intentionally signing the wrong form. The rest of the group will then be asked to sign *yes* or *no* to indicate whether or not the student is signing the correct form.

VARIATION   The fingerspelling of the homophone can be substituted for the sign.

EVALUATION   The student will be given unlined paper and asked to illustrate the meaning of the homophones being studied. A sentence will also be written for each homophone.

Lesson 35/SPELLING

LEVEL   Intermediate

MATERIALS   Spelling list

OBJECTIVE   Given a spelling or other language arts generality and a spelling list, the student will find an example of that generality.

FUNCTION OF TOTAL COMMUNICATION IN LESSON
Tactile/kinesthetic learning

LETTERS AND SIGNS NEEDED
Alphabet (see Lesson 3)

PROCEDURE   The teacher will tell the class members that they will be having a word search using the spelling list. The children will be asked to find various kinds of words. When a child finds a word for the generality, he or she will fingerspell it. Some sample search tasks are, "Find a word that"

1. Ends in silent "e."
2. Has two syllables.
3. Means more than one of something.
4. Is a compound word.
5. Has a long "a."
6. Starts with a blend.
7. Is an adjective.
8. Has a prefix.

Of course, only tasks that relate to the current list should be chosen.

VARIATION   This activity may be used in a classroom in which all members have the same list or in a class in which lists differ. If lists vary from child to child, a student who does not have a word to fit the generality can sign *no*.

Lesson 36/RECOGNIZING COMPLETE SENTENCES

LEVEL   Intermediate

MATERIALS   None

OBJECTIVE   Given an answer to a question, the student will sign *sentence* or *no* to indicate whether the answer is a sentence.

FUNCTION OF TOTAL COMMUNICATION IN LESSON
Every pupil response

LETTERS AND SIGNS NEEDED

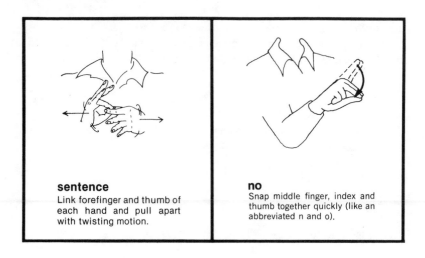

sentence
Link forefinger and thumb of each hand and pull apart with twisting motion.

no
Snap middle finger, index and thumb together quickly (like an abbreviated n and o).

PROCEDURE   The teacher will introduce complete sentences, giving and soliciting examples. He or she will tell the class that they will be playing a sentence game. The teacher will ask a question concerning anything of interest to the students. A volunteer can answer the question. If the student answers in a complete sentence, the class will sign *sentence*. If the answer is not a sentence, the class will sign *no*. For instance, the teacher might ask, "What time is recess?" A student might answer, "Ten o'clock." In that case, the group would sign *no*, whereas, if the child had answered, "Recess is at ten o'clock." the class would sign *sentence*.

(Before play begins, the children should be encouraged to mix their answers, that is, to avoid a pattern of using all sentence or all nonsentence answers for the game.)

VARIATION   After the group is familiar with the game, children can play it in pairs.

EVALUATION   The teacher can ask questions such as, "What is your favorite color?" Children can be asked to write a complete sentence answer.

Lesson 37/CREATIVE THINKING

LEVEL   Advanced/gifted

MATERIALS   Magazines

OBJECTIVE   The student will explore the importance of nonverbal communication symbols in advertising a product.

LETTERS AND SIGNS NEEDED
None

PROCEDURE   The class will briefly play the game, Simon Says, and then discuss the importance of nonverbal clues. Many players make false moves because they respond to the leader's nonverbal clues rather than verbal ones. The game illustrates that "Actions speak louder than words," or that visual clues are stronger many times than auditory ones.

The class can be led into a discussion of how this fact is used in advertising. A few examples from a magazine can be shown. Nonverbal communication in TV commercials should be discussed. For example, the commercial for Haley's M.O. has used the A-OK hand gesture to promote their product.

The students can be assigned to watch TV or read printed material for two or three sessions. Their purpose will be to collect samples of use of nonverbal gestures in ads. The results will be explored using questions such as the following: Would the ads be as effective if nonverbal communication were not used? Can you think of a better gesture to sell the product?

As an additional activity students can prepare magazine ads and TV (videotaped) ads emphasizing use of gestures.

Lesson 38/CREATIVE THINKING

LEVEL   Advanced

MATERIALS   None

OBJECTIVE   Given a theme, the student will practice dramatic expression through a modified version of the game of charades.

LETTERS AND SIGNS NEEDED

None

PROCEDURE   The class will work in two teams. Each member of the teams will be given a number. When the student's number is called, she or he must act out the theme given by the teacher. (The teacher should be sure all the students will be familiar with the themes used. They can be one-word titles of books, games, or TV shows.)

This game is not based on syllable guessing like the traditional game of charades. Rather, pantomiming the ideas or words is the method used. For each correct guess, the team gains one point. The time limit for acting out the word or words is to be only 2 or 3 minutes. If, at the end of the time, the team has not guessed the answer, the game is continued with the opposing team.

Lesson 39/CREATIVE THINKING

LEVEL   Advanced/gifted

MATERIALS   Pictures of international symbols, such as restaurant or hospital; list of word to be illustrated, paper, pencil, crayons

OBJECTIVE   The student will express an idea through alternative methods, that is, drawing a picture or using a sign.

LETTERS AND SIGNS NEEDED

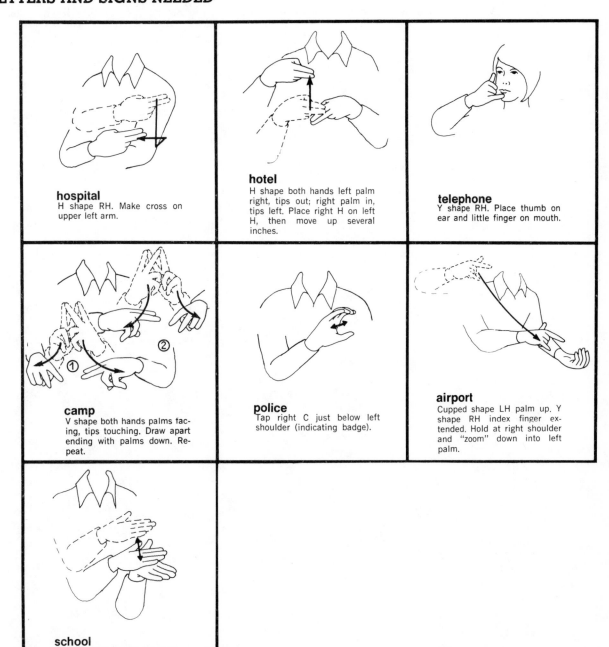

hospital
H shape RH. Make cross on upper left arm.

hotel
H shape both hands left palm right, tips out; right palm in, tips left. Place right H on left H, then move up several inches.

telephone
Y shape RH. Place thumb on ear and little finger on mouth.

camp
V shape both hands palms facing, tips touching. Draw apart ending with palms down. Repeat.

police
Tap right C just below left shoulder (indicating badge).

airport
Cupped shape LH palm up. Y shape RH index finger extended. Hold at right shoulder and "zoom" down into left palm.

school
Open B both hands, left palm up, tips out; right palm down, tips left. Clap together.

PROCEDURE   The teacher will discuss with the class the advantages and necessity of using international symbols (in view of language barriers, ease of reading, and illiteracy). The class will look at an example of an international symbol. The teacher will direct each student to create an international symbol for a word. The illustrations will be collected and class members will guess what idea each communicates.

Next, the sign language signs for each word will be demonstrated with students trying to guess what word is being signed. (The word iconic can be introduced.) The class can discuss which signs are iconic. The signs can be compared to the illustrations. How are they similar? Which are easier to understand? What is the possibility of inventing an international sign system for communicating? What would be the advantages? What would the obstacles be? (*GESTUNO* by the World Federation of the Deaf is a book on international sign language. It is available for $16.50 at the Sign Language Store (see Appendix A). Another resource for this lesson is the Milton Bradley Signs and Symbols flashcards.)

LEARNING CENTER ACTIVITIES

The following seven activities are suggestions for Total Communication Approach learning centers (Figure 10).

Activity 1/ALPHABET

LEVEL   Readiness/Primary

MATERIALS   Oak tag, manila folder, felt-tip pens

OBJECTIVE   Given the manual clues, the student will match them with printed letters of the alphabet.

FUNCTION OF TOTAL COMMUNICATION
Tactile/kinesthetic learning

LETTERS AND SIGNS NEEDED
Student Sheet 1 (see Appendix B)

PROCEDURE   The teacher will draw a dachshund on oak tag or the inside of a manila folder. The letters of the printed alphabet will be on individual cards which fit in between the head and tail of the dog. Children will match cards with the manual alphabet letter to the printed letters. A pocket to store the cards should be included. The teacher will also make a "bone" for each student.

The student will pull a letter card, make the manual alphabet letter for the printed letter and place the card on the appropriate space on the dog.

A score sheet on the front of the folder can be included to provide a way for the student to record her or his progress. When the student scores 100%, he or she will be awarded a bone.

VARIATION   A few of the letters can be presented at a time. As students learn more letters, they can be added to the dog.

Activity 2/DOLCH SIGHT WORD VOCABULARY

LEVEL   Primary

MATERIALS   Word cards

OBJECTIVE   Given a self checking deck of cards, the student will practice reading sight words.

FUNCTION OF TOTAL COMMUNICATION
Tactile/kinesthetic learning

LETTERS AND SIGNS NEEDED
Student Sheet 2 (see Appendix B)

Figure 10. Students at a sign language learning center work independently. The student on the left is reading a book from the Signed English Series while the student on the right is matching sight vocabulary with the corresponding signs.

PROCEDURE The teacher will prepare a deck of Total Communication cards by reproducing and cutting out the sign cards on the Student Sheet. (Each may be pasted to an index card to make a sturdier deck.)

These will be available in a center where a child can go to practice sight words with another student or aide. The child will look at one card at a time. He or she will make the sign for the word and read it to the partner. After the child is able to read the words while looking at the signed clue, the partner can cover the sign and direct the child to read the printed word alone. If he or she needs a clue, the sign can be uncovered.

VARIATION Other sight word lists or vocabulary from basal readers can be used.

Activity 3/RHYMING WORDS

LEVEL Primary/Intermediate

MATERIALS Language Master and cards, table-standing mirror

OBJECTIVE Given a series of rhyming words orally, the student will fingerspell the words.

FUNCTION OF TOTAL COMMUNICATION
Tactile/kinesthetic learning

LETTERS AND SIGNS NEEDED
Student Sheet 3 (see Appendix B)

PROCEDURE On each Language Master card, the teacher will record two or three rhyming words that are similar in spelling, for instance, *hat—rat—cat*, on track 1. On the back of the card, the teacher will attach the printed version of the rhyming words.

    The student will be directed to listen to the card and then fingerspell the rhyming words into the mirror as he or she repeats the words. The student will experience rhyming multisensorially. The work can be checked by turning to the back of the card.

Activity 4/SPELLING

LEVEL Primary/Intermediate

MATERIALS Table-standing mirror, Language Master and cards

OBJECTIVE Given a list of words, the student will use auditory, visual, and kinesthetic input to practice the spelling of the words.

FUNCTION OF TOTAL COMMUNICATION
Tactile/kinesthetic learning

SIGNS AND LETTERS NEEDED
Student Sheet 3 (see Appendix B)

PROCEDURE The teacher will record one spelling word on each Language Master card. On the back of the card, he or she will attach the printed version of the recorded word. The student will listen to the word and fingerspell it into the mirror. (The student is then concentrating on the visual and kinesthetic aspects of the word after having concentrated on the auditory aspect.) The student will check his or her answer on the back of the card.

VARIATION The teacher may instruct the student to first concentrate on the visual aspect of the word only. The student then closes his or her eyes and concentrates on the kinesthetic aspect of the word.

Activity 5/SPELLING WORDS

LEVEL Primary/Intermediate

MATERIALS Colored oak tag, construction paper, felt-tip pens

OBJECTIVE Given a list of spelling words, the student will correctly spell each word before putting the spelling eggs in the basket.

FUNCTION OF TOTAL COMMUNICATION
Tactile/kinesthetic learning

LETTERS AND SIGNS NEEDED
Student Sheet 4 (see Appendix B)

PROCEDURE Each student will make an egg basket by cutting out and decorating the basket shape on the Student Sheet. Each child's basket will be placed on a bulletin board. They should be stapled to form a pocket.

Whenever spelling words are introduced, the students will cut out large paper eggs and put a spelling word on each. When the student has free time, she or he can use the spelling eggs and fingerspelling to practice the words. In this manner, the student can practice spelling words quietly and also benefit from using the tactile/kinesthetic sense.

After weekly spelling tests are given, the students put the words they spelled correctly into the baskets. The words misspelled are retained for further practice. Periodically, the teacher can pull the students' eggs and use them for a review.

Activity 6/EXPRESSIVE LANGUAGE AND CREATIVE WRITING

LEVEL Intermediate

MATERIALS Polaroid camera, words cards (glad, sad, afraid, nervous, angry, calm, curious) and a mirror

OBJECTIVE Given words for emotions, the student will match the word with its illustration, write a sentence for the emotion and read the sentence expressively.

FUNCTION OF TOTAL COMMUNICATION
Illustrate concept

LETTERS AND SIGNS NEEDED
See Lesson Plan 29 (Chapter 4)

PROCEDURE Students will be photographed making the signs for the emotion words. The photos and word cards will be placed in a learning center. Students visiting the center will be asked to match the pictures with the words. They will then be directed to write a sentence for each emotion. For example, "Pat was *sad* when the new toy broke." After writing the seven sentences, the students will read them expressively while watching facial expressiveness in the mirror.

Activity 7/FACT–FANTASY

LEVEL   Intermediate

MATERIALS   Sentence strips, paper clips

FUNCTION OF TOTAL COMMUNICATION
Motivation

LETTERS AND SIGNS NEEDED
Student Sheet 5 (see Appendix B)

PROCEDURE   The teacher will write a real (fact) or impossible (fantasy) statement on each sentence strip. Cards with *real* and *can't* must be cut from the Student Sheet 5. The cards should be placed in an envelope with some paper clips.

       The student will be directed to read each sentence and use paper clips to attach a card with either a *real* or *can't* on it to each. Work can be evaluated by checking a key or answers put on the back of the strips.

VARIATION   After the student has completed the exercise, he or she can write real and impossible statements on extra sentence strips and leave them at the center for others to use.

SONG, STORIES, AND POEMS IN SIGN LANGUAGE

Combining sign language with familiar songs, stories, and poems is an effective way to enhance the students' enjoyment of this important part of the language arts program.

Signing familiar stories helps to develop listening skills. The child must watch and attend or she or he misses the story. If the student has to focus both visually and aurally on a story, distraction by other stimulus in the room will not be a problem.

A good approach to signing a story is signing the key words or the words that the teacher judges should be emphasized, for example, the italicized words should be signed from this line of *Little Red Riding Hood*, "The *better* to *eat* you with my *dear!*"

This selective approach to signing allows the student to focus on the words that carry the meaning of the story, thereby helping to develop skimming skills as well. Signing one or two words in a sentence ensures that the child will see the sign. If the teacher signed all the words (an impossibility for anyone who is not fluent in sign), it would be difficult for the students to assimilate the signs.

After the teacher has signed the story, song, or poem through once, the children should be encouraged to copy the signs or to sign them along with the teacher.

Songs are especially fun and easy to learn. The teacher should start with a song the children know. Later, after the class has built up a sign vocabulary, new songs can be attempted. The signs seem to help students learn new song lyrics more quickly. Learning to sign and sing holiday songs is a special treat for children. Songs that the children learn can be incorporated into PTA programs or other performances.

In schools where deaf children are mainstreamed, there are extra benefits. Seldom do deaf children really participate in the programs for parents. Their participation is usually limited to a token walk-on part. In a sign chorus, they have just as important a part as everyone else. It also gives them a chance to help other children learn a new skill at which they are already expert.

Signing stories and songs is especially beneficial when expression in dramatic reading is to be emphasized. The very nature of sign language encourages the child to use more body language and facial and voice expression. Drastic changes have been noted in everyday gestures and facial expressions of young hearing children who have been exposed to Total Communication.

Total Communication in conjunction with videotaping is also strongly suggested. Together these tools can be helpful in developing expressive language.

Below is a brief list of stories, songs, and poems that are a good start; however, anything can be signed. The *Signed English Series* listed in Appendix A is also an excellent source for stories. These are written in sign and print and can be used in groups or individually in library corners to build vocabulary. An exciting additional benefit is that after a student learns a sign she or he will connect the sign with the printed word while looking at the book and effortlessly begin to read the actual word.

STORIES

Little Red Riding Hood
The Gingerbread Man
The Three Billy Goats Gruff
Goldilocks and the Three Bears

POEMS/FINGERPLAYS

Jack and Jill
Humpty Dumpty
Star Wish ("Star light, star bright, first star I see this night...")
The Eensy, Weensy Spider

SONGS

Twinkle, Twinkle Little Star
The Good Morning Song
Happy Birthday
Three Blind Mice

GAMES

Of course, not every moment has to be devoted to language arts lessons. Sometimes, the alert teacher sees that it is time for a change of pace. He or she sees that the children will work more effectively if refreshed with a quick game or puzzle or activity. The following Total Communication games provide ideas for those in-between or restless minutes.

Most of the games are sign language versions of familiar games so it will not take long for the children to learn the rules. Also, student sheets in Appendix B make it possible for the teacher to duplicate sets of the signs children will need and keep them handy so that the games will be ready when needed.

BINGO (STUDENT SHEET 3)

The students will fold scrap paper so that there are four boxes across and down. The students will randomly fill the card by printing a letter of the alphabet in each box. The caller will make manual alphabet letters. If a student has the letter made by the caller, she or he may put an X in the box. Play continues until one player has four in a row.

NAME GAME RELAY (STUDENT SHEET 3)

The class will be divided into several equal groups. Each group will stand in a line. At the signal, the first student will turn to the second and fingerspell his or her name as quickly as possible. The second student will then turn to the third and fingerspell his or her name and so forth until the last student has spelled at which point the entire line will raise their hands and make the "V" or victory sign.

ALPHATRICK (STUDENT SHEET 3)

The teacher will ask the students the following riddles. The students will make the manual alphabet letter that answers the riddle.

Which letter is an insect?   (B)
Which letter is a vegetable?   (P)
Which letter is a bird?   (J)
Which letter do you use to see?   (I)
Which letter is a name for someone else?   (U)
Which letter is a question?   (Y)
Which letter is a drink?   (T)
Which letter means you have to pay someone?   (O)

SCRABBLE (STUDENT SHEET 6)

An ordinary Scrabble board and rules are used. The "tiles" are the manual alphabet letters on the Student Sheet.

HANG IT (STUDENT SHEET 6)

The rules are similar to those for Hangman. The students will work in groups of two or three. Each group will be furnished a large piece of paper. The traditional Hangman set up should be prepared on the paper.

One student thinks of a word and draws the appropriate number of blanks to represent the word. The other students in the group must guess letters that may be needed to spell the word. Instead of saying the letters, the guessing students will show the letters using the manual alphabet.

If a student guesses a correct letter, the manual alphabet letter for that letter (from the Student Sheet) should be placed on the proper blank. If the guess is incorrect, the letter should be displayed near the Hang It platform and one body part drawn. Students will try to spell or guess the word before a complete body is formed.

FIND THE LEADER (STUDENT SHEET 7)

Student A will be sent out of the room. Student B will be named group leader. He or she will lead the class in making the signs for the days of the week. Student A will return. The class then follows the lead of Student B in making signs. For instance, he or she may decide to make the sign for Tuesday several times, the sign for Friday several times, and so forth. Student A will observe and try to identify the group leader. Once identified, the leader will then become the student who must guess the new leader.

I SAY SIGN (STUDENT SHEET 8)

The rules for this game are like the ones for Simon Says. The teacher will sign directions to the class. If the direction is prefaced with the sign for *I say*, the students do the action.

WHO STOLE THE COOKIE IN SIGN (STUDENT SHEET 9)

Each child is assigned a number. The children recite the familiar "Who Stole the Cookie?" Instead of clapping and chanting, as is traditional, they will sign as they chant the words.

Class: Who stole the cookie from the cookie jar?
Teacher: Number 6 stole the cookie from the cookie jar.
Number 6:   Who, me?
Class: Yes, you.
Number 6:   Can't be.
Class: Then who?
Number 6:   Number 3 stole the cookie from the cookie jar.
Number 3:   Who, me? (Continue as above.)

TOY STORE (STUDENT SHEET 10)

Each student will have a turn to sign the statement, "I went to the store to get a _____." As each takes her or his turn, a new toy will be added to the list. Example:

A.   I went to the store to get a boat.
B.   I went to the store to get a boat and a ball.

I SEE RED (STUDENT SHEET 11)

One student is chosen to be leader. She or he signs, "I see red (or any color)." The rest of the students try to guess the object the leader is thinking of. The student who guesses correctly becomes the new leader. (The answers can be given orally or students can use signs they know and homemade signs for their guesses, if desired.)

RHYMES, JOKES, AND SONGS (ADVANCED)

Children can practice translating well known jump-rope rhymes, short songs, or brief jokes into sign if a dictionary of sign such as *The Signed English Dictionary* is provided. Those who succeed can be asked to perform for the class or be videotaped and shown to the group at a later time.

FAST WORDS (ADVANCED)

One student is appointed leader. He or she signs a letter. The student who is taking a turn must sign as many words as possible that start with that letter. A turn lasts 1 minute. One point may be scored for each word if score is to be kept. Students may fingerspell or sign.

CHAPTER 5
ADDITIONAL BENEFITS OF THE TOTAL COMMUNICATION APPROACH

The Total Communication Approach tries harder. It facilitates language arts instruction but it also has other beneficial effects. They are by-products of the student's interest and knowledge of some letters and signs and require no extra effort by the teacher.

KEEPING A GROUP'S ATTENTION

The Total Communication Approach can even be effective in some of those perennial "tough cookie" situations dreaded by new teachers and still pondered by retired ones. One of these is keeping each child involved in whole class instruction. Large group instruction is often like fitting an oddly shaped package in a box. As soon as one side is secure, the other pops out. A class lesson can be fine for 5 seconds and then Billy starts to stare out the window. The teacher walks over to Billy so he will attend, and then Sally who is sitting eight desks away starts to play with something in her desk. The teacher catches Sally's eye, and then Pete starts to pass a note, and so it goes.

One of the problems inherent in group instruction is too much "down time" for students. There is more waiting and listening than participating. It is hard for the child who is bursting with the answer to a question to sit quietly and wait for a turn, or worse, not get a turn.

On the other hand, it is easy for a student who is having problems to get lost in the crowd. Children quickly learn how to hide behind the big guy so the teacher won't ask for an answer when a difficult skill is being practiced.

Using the Total Communication Approach alleviates these group instruction shortcomings. When signs and fingerspelling are used, every student actively responds. No one's mind or fingers can wander because each is using hand and mind to participate. The child is not an observer. She or he is totally involved.

Nor can students hide from participation, and thereby, compound confusion or problems they may be having. The teacher can instantly see which children are faltering and give immediate extra help.

MANAGING STUDENT BEHAVIOR

Another side benefit of using the Total Communication Approach is that signs can help teachers manage students' behavior effectively and positively.

It is common knowledge that inappropriate behavior on a child's part is often a cry for attention. The humane teacher wants to respond to this need for love and attention and yet cannot leave a reading group of ten to give a child a pat on the shoulder when he or she starts loudly tapping a pencil.

Often, the attention comes in the form of a sharp, "Sit down, and get back to your work!" Signs can come to the rescue. Teachers have found it effective to flash a "hi" or better yet, an "I love you" (Figure 11) sign to the child. They report that, generally, the child will grin and get back to work. Such handling of a minor classroom disturbance does not interrupt the teacher's work with the group and gives the attention seeker extra reinforcement to get back on track. Even in the cases where subsequent action must be taken, the teacher loses nothing by trying this step first. On the contrary, the child will know that the teacher cares even if a reprimand is forthcoming.

Smoothly Running Classrooms

New teachers often say they are not as scared about the big details such as teaching reading and making math centers as they are afraid of tripping over the little things. And 5 years later, as seasoned professionals they are still trying to find the perfect system for dealing with mundane considerations like lining up and bathroom procedure.

Some of these bothersome details can be streamlined through using signs. Instead of designing elaborate systems for leaving the room, a flash of a sign can do the trick. When a child wants to ask permission to leave, he or she can simply sign "b" for bathroom, "w" for water fountain, "l" for library or whatever is appropriate. The teacher can acknowledge by signing *yes* without interrupting instruction or disturbing students who are working.

Signs can also be used for simple directions like *line up*, *stop*, or *quiet*. These are particularly helpful when the class is settling from a noisy activity or in the cafeteria. It is more pleasant and professional to make oneself "heard" in sign rather than scream across the clatter of knives, forks, and excited voices.

The children who are looking and receive the direction can pass it along to those sitting near them by repeating the sign. In a matter of seconds, the message can be communicated.

I LOVE YOU

(the letter I-L-Y)

Figure 11.   I love you sign.

Cooperative Spirit

As one offshoot of using the Total Communication Approach, children learn a new and useful skill...the ability to make some signs. This skill can enhance individual self concept. Children using signs in their language arts program are "privileged characters." They are learning something fun that a lot of other people do not know. They are not being babied, but rather doing something that some adults do, and better, that many adults do not know how to do. They are the envy of their schoolmates. "What are you doing? Wow! Show me how to do it!" In some situations, children who are usually stigmatized because of a learning problem have learned some signs and then been sought after by average and high achievers who want to learn the skill.

Knowing something interesting that others may not know as well as progressing in language arts can and often does make a child feel better about school and self.

Additionally, class spirit can develop. The class using the Total Communication Approach is the class that gets to "do the fun stuff" to learn language. Also, the class benefits from more partner learning and more effective, pleasant large group experiences.

Difficult Moments

The teacher who becomes familiar with signs will find that they are helpful in difficult moments such as class dismissal. It is both calming and fun, for instance, to tell the class that their initials will be made in the manual alphabet. When they see their own, they may get their coats and get ready to leave. The teacher can challenge the students to repeat everyone's initials.

Learning signs for fun and vocabulary enrichment is a pleasant way to fill in those odd moments when the music teacher is 5 minutes late or another teacher says, "Will you step into my room while I make a phone call?" For slightly longer blocks of time, the games and activities in Chapter 4 provide active but not nerve-wracking change of pace and positive experiences for using language skills.

Open Space

The Total Communication Approach has a particular benefit relating to behavior in open classroom situations. Often, teachers feel inhibited when other classes and teachers are working nearby. They hesitate to initiate a spelling relay, sight word bingo, or other game-type lessons for fear the excitement will disturb others. The Total Communication Approach addresses this concern in animating children in a quiet way.

Home/School Relations

Whenever parents become enthusiastic about school, the parent/child/teacher triangle of concern is completed and everyone benefits. Because parent support is vital, it is a teacher's job to include parents in the curriculum. The use of a Total Communication Approach will interest parents in their child's education.

Some parents will be intrigued when they see their child using fingerspelling to study spelling words or see her or him teaching signs to a neighborhood friend. Even better, the teacher can send a note home telling parents of the new method being used in the class (see Student Sheet 12).

Perhaps a copy of the manual alphabet or some signs would spark parent interest. An example of how the Total Communication Approach can be used to teach a language arts lesson can be demonstrated at a PTA meeting.

Later, when some children's interest extends beyond the letters and signs used in language arts lessons, sheets of interest words (such as holiday signs taken from a sign language dictionary) and games that use fingerspelling or signs can be sent home for family use.

In some classes using the Total Communication Approach, parents have become so intrigued that they have bought sign language books or taken courses to learn the language as a family project. In one class in which lack of parent interest had previously been a severe problem, some parents made their first contact with the school to tell the teacher they liked having their children learning signs.

When parent interest and curiosity are aroused, some may volunteer to practice with children who want to learn additional signs for fun.

Mainstreaming

Mainstreaming is currently being implemented in public schools. The proponents of the concept, which is now mandated by law, believe it is healthy for children who have physical differences, such as deafness, to learn in the least restrictive environment possible. The teacher using a Total Communication Approach has an advantage in a mainstreaming situation involving deaf or hearing-impaired students.

More important, the children would be more comfortable. The hearing children would not regard the signs of the deaf children as strange. The deaf students might feel less apprehensive if new classmates were familiar with the manual alphabet and a few signs. For many deaf children, sign language is the major means of communication. If hearing children also know it, the deaf child has a chance of social participation and is not isolated from classmates.

Understanding of the Deaf

For the hearing user of signs, there comes a greater understanding and awareness of those who use American Sign Language, the third most widely used language in the United States. The ability to communicate even minimally with a deaf individual is one source of this understanding and pride.

Some teachers may feel that they want to go a little farther because invariably students get excited about the Total Communication Approach and want to know more signs than the few used in the language arts lessons. A book that teaches basic and frequently used signs is helpful. Several are listed in Appendix A.

Some teachers will be intellectually fascinated by signs and fingerspelling and want to know more for their own information and for those children for whom signs become an extracurricular activity. There are short courses in introductory sign language offered through adult education centers, churches, community colleges, and schools for the deaf. Some elementary, middle, and high schools already offer sign language as an elective minicourse. It may be possible to have someone teach a brief course in the school if several people are interested. A check with the National Association of the Deaf, a community college, or a local school for the deaf should help identify resource people.

If the classroom teacher is interested in this "widening horizons" aspect, a meeting of hearing and deaf students can be arranged.

A class of deaf children (preferably a small class) can be invited to visit. Careful attention to details will ensure success. An interpreter (who may be the visiting teacher if she or he signs and hears) is needed. Before the visit, the teacher of the hearing class should prepare the children for the fact that some of the visitors will be learning to speak, but may be hard to understand.

The teacher can have children explore the reason for this difficulty in speech. A quick exercise can show the difficulty of learning speech without hearing. Each child should be directed to turn to another. At a signal, one child will block both ears with his or her fingers. The other will make up a word and say it very softly. The child with the blocked ears will try to repeat the word. The difficulty of speech under such circumstances and reasons for it can be discussed briefly in terms of a deaf child learning to talk. If the teacher takes a few minutes in such an exercise, it is more likely that the students will not be stunned by the deaf children's speech, but admire the accomplishment.

The activities for the visit should be planned. For instance, in one such visit, the teacher of the deaf children using both speech and signs, told a story to a group of hearing and deaf students. She also shared a guessing game with them. The experience ended with a question and answer period in which children were given a chance, through the interpreter, to ask questions about each other's schools.

Many teachers may be apprehensive about this type of activity. Those who try it, however, will find that watching the exciting moment when the deaf and hearing children stop being nervous about each other and start being "just kids" enjoying a story together may be the most rewarding of the school year.

Hopefully, the experience will extend into the community. Traditionally, some deaf people have been hesitant to use signs in public. They have not wanted to bring attention to themselves or arouse curiosity. Lately, this attitude has changed.

The teacher who uses the Total Communication Approach may find that children are soon sharing stories about having seen people in the community signing. One shy child who had been exposed to signs in language arts class came bursting into the classroom one morning to tell her teacher she had seen two people signing in the grocery store. The child walked up to them forgetting her shyness, and signed, *hi*. This simple event boosted her self-concept and gave evidence to the deaf couple that the hearing members of the community are becoming more aware and open.

The teacher who decides to go beyond using the Total Communication Approach for language arts instruction will find there is much ignorance in relation to deafness. Most children and adults simply have not had contact with people who do not hear. A fuller awareness can come if a deaf adult and an interpreter

visit the class. Another alternative is to invite a person who works with the deaf such as a teacher or librarian. That person should have the background to answer questions and share materials, such as stories and books in sign. In classes where this has been done, the teacher soon becomes aware of the need for this give and take of information when children ask questions such as, "Can deaf children ride bikes?"

Through this type of communication, students will learn that *deaf* does not mean *dumb*, in either sense of the word. Lack of hearing does not indicate intellectual inferiority. The class will also learn that deafness does imply some differences. They will realize, however, that if alternate ways of doing such things as using a telephone and watching television are made available, *deaf* does not mean *disabled*.

Although learning signs and fingerspelling makes it easier for hearing people to share with deaf people, it means the converse is true also. There are many things which deaf people have to share with hearing people.

Signs themselves are a gift from the deaf community. They are fun, expressive, and challenging. They teach the user to be more animated and open to others. The telling of a story in sign can be a dramatic experience that enthralls both children and adults. A class visit to a performance by a drama group from a local school for the deaf is an exciting experience.

As the teacher and class become more aware of deafness and signs, they will have the key to many experiences previously locked to them.

A FINAL NOTE

Now that you have read this book, you are equipped to use the Total Communication Approach. You will probably start by using one of the prepared lessons in Chapter 4. Once you have become satisfied that the Total Communication Approach does facilitate teaching some language arts skills at your grade level, you will probably branch off and find other ways to use it.

Some of the teachers who find the Total Communication Approach useful in teaching will find time to enhance their curriculum by introducing students to a more indepth understanding of the language and special contributions of the 13.4 million Americans who are deaf or hearing impaired.

The Total Communication Approach has been introduced to make language arts easier and more fun to teach in an effective manner. Use it any way that helps your students.

Please feel free to share this new approach with other teachers and students.

APPENDIX A
RESOURCES

RESOURCES HELPFUL IN
THE TOTAL COMMUNICATION CLASSROOM

AVAILABLE FROM THE FOLLOWING SOURCES:

GCB

Gallaudet College Bookstore
Gallaudet College
Washington, D. C. 20009

NAD

National Association of the Deaf
814 Thayer Avenue
Silver Spring, Maryland 20910

JMP

Joyce Motion Picture Co.
8613 Yolanda Avenue
P.O. Box 458
Northridge, California 91328

SLS

Sign Language Store
8613 Yolanda Avenue
P.O. Box 4440
Northridge, California 91328

TJP

T. J. Publishers, Inc.
1817 Silver Spring Avenue
Silver Spring, Md. 20910

UPP

University Park Press
300 North Charles Street
Baltimore, Maryland 21201

NAD   *A Basic Course in Manual Communication*, O'Rourke, $5.75. Beginning sign language book containing 737 signs.

TJP   *A Basic Vocabulary of American Sign Language for Parents and Children*, O'Rourke, $12.95 hard, $8.95 paper. Contains 1,150 signs used especially by parents and children.

JMP   *Sign Language for Everyone*, State Department of Health, $12.95

GCB   *Talk With Your Hands*, Watson, $5.75. Book includes short explanation of signs.

GCB   *The Joy of Signing*, Riekehof, $12.95. A dictionary of 1,300 signs with origin of sign and synonym indicated.

GCB
Signed English Series. A series of books and posters intended to teach English to deaf children through a modification of sign language. These are useful for Total Communication instruction in the regular classroom.

Jack and the Beanstalk	$ 4.00
Little Red Riding Hood	2.50
Hansel and Gretel	3.50
The Night Before Christmas	3.50
Little Poems for Little People	3.50
Three Billy Goats Gruff	3.00
Song in Signed English	3.00
Nursery Rhymes from Mother Goose	3.50
Signed English in the Classroom	4.00
(a reference of common signs used in the classroom)	
Signed English Dictionary	15.00

GCB
Sign Language Made Simple, Lawrence, $8.95. A layperson's guide to learning sign language.

NAD
Note Pads, 200 sheets, $2.25
"I Love You" symbol
"Happy Hands, Happy Hearts"
"Let Your Fingers Do the Talking"
"Stop Noise Pollution, Use Sign Language"

NAD
You've Got A Song, Gadling & Pokorny, $2.00. Selected popular songs including melody line, chords, words and pictures of signed translation.

NAD
Coloring Books in Sign, $2.50 each. Topics include animals, home, community, and food.

NAD
International Hand Alphabet Charts, Carmel $3.95. A book of illustrations of hand alphabets from over 30 countries.

NAD
Manual Alphabet Poster, I Love You Gift Co., $2.25, 21" x 25½". Colorful poster featuring unique characters performing each letter of the alphabet.

JMP
All of the following were printed by Hallmark Cards, Inc., Kansas City, Mo.
Fun Days, holidays children love in signed English, $3.50.
Animal Antics, a first counting book in sign, $3.50.
Great Big Fire Engine Book, a Golden Book in sign, $3.50.
The Toy Book, a Golden Shape Book, sign language version, $1.50.
The Dog Book, a Golden Shape Book in sign, $1.50.

Animal Antics, Fun Days, plus other books are available in film cartridges, $6.95 each.

SLS
I Love You stamp, Joyce Media, $7.95. Self-inking stamp to correct papers or reward good work (red ink).

SLS
110 School Survival Signs, Joyce Media Co., $1.60 for 10. 10 mini-dictionaries per package. Designed for mainstream programs.

SLS
Sign Language Flashcards, Hoemann, $6.25, contains 500 flashcards with over 1,000 signs.

SLS
Alphabet Wall Cards, Joyce Media Co., $8.95. Large, white stock, 11" x 12" with black lettering, one card for every letter of the alphabet.

SLS	Keep Quiet, $7.05. A fingerspelling crossword cube game that teaches the manual alphabet.
SLS	Sign Language rubber stamp set, Joyce Media, Inc. $35.95. 26 rubber stamps, one for each manual alphabet letter.
SLS	*Communication Carousel*, Buchanan & Harlow, $14.95. A text of activities, games and suggestions for teaching the manual alphabet to hearing-impaired and perceptually impaired children. All pages are reproducible.
SLS	*Play It By Sign*, Kirchner, $12.95. 26 games to aid teaching the manual alphabet.
SLS	*Signs for All Seasons*, Kirchner, $11.65. 50 sign language games.
SLS	*Games and Activities*, Royster, $3.50. A guide for creating games and activities in sign.
GCB	*Gestures*, Miles, $6.95. Poetry in sign language.

FOR CHILDREN WHO WANT TO KNOW MORE ABOUT SIGN LANGUAGE

NAD	*Ben's Quiet World*, $.60. Ben's hearing sister explains to her friends all about Ben's speech, hearing, and his signs.
NAD	*The Girl Who Wouldn't Talk*, Goldfeder, $3.50. A charming story about a little deaf girl named Robin and the problems she faces growing up in a world where everyone talks. The story shows how Robin learns to talk through sign language.
NAD	*A Button in Her Ear*, Litchfield, $5.75, Albert Whitman & Co. A little girl relates how her hearing problem is detected and corrected through the use of a hearing aid.
NAD	*I Have a Sister, My Sister is Deaf*, Petersen, $4.95, Harper & Row. Warm, intimate pictures and a poetic text evoke an appealing and perceptive portrait of a young deaf child.
UPP	*Manual Communication: A Basic Text and Workbook with Practical Exercises*, Christopher, $17.50. More than 800 signs taught with clear illustration and plenty of practice pages.
NAD	*Robin Sees a Song*, Pahz, $3.75. One night a little deaf girl is visited by a song and learns an important lesson. This story is a beautiful fantasy for children.

FOR TEACHERS WHO WANT TO KNOW MORE ABOUT SIGN LANGUAGE AND DEAFNESS

NAD	*They Grow in Silence*, Mindel & Vernon, $5.50. Examines the problems that deaf children and their parents face.
NAD	*Education of the Deaf: Psychology, Principles and Practices*, Moores, $14.95, Houghton Mifflin Co. Covers the historical development and current state of the art. Topics include causes of deafness, manual communication, educational programs and more.
NAD	*In This Sign*, Greenberg, $5.95, Holt, Rhinehart, Winston. Illustrates the problems of a young, deaf couple during the Depression.

APPENDIX B
STUDENT SHEETS

These student worksheets are provided for the convenience of the teacher. All sheets may be reproduced as necessary for classroom use.

Student Sheet 1

a	b	c	d	e
f	g	h	i	j
k	l	m	n	o
p	q	r	s	t

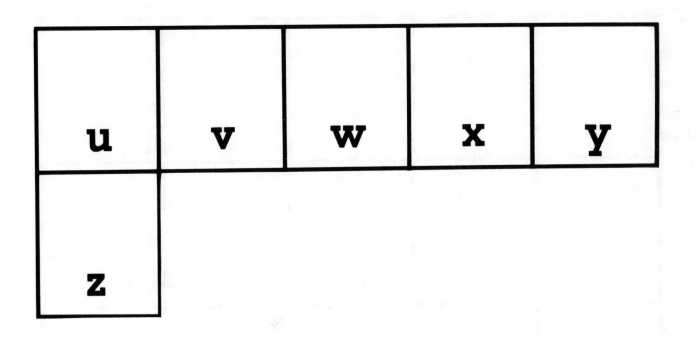

u	v	w	x	y
z				

continued

Student Sheet 1—*continued*

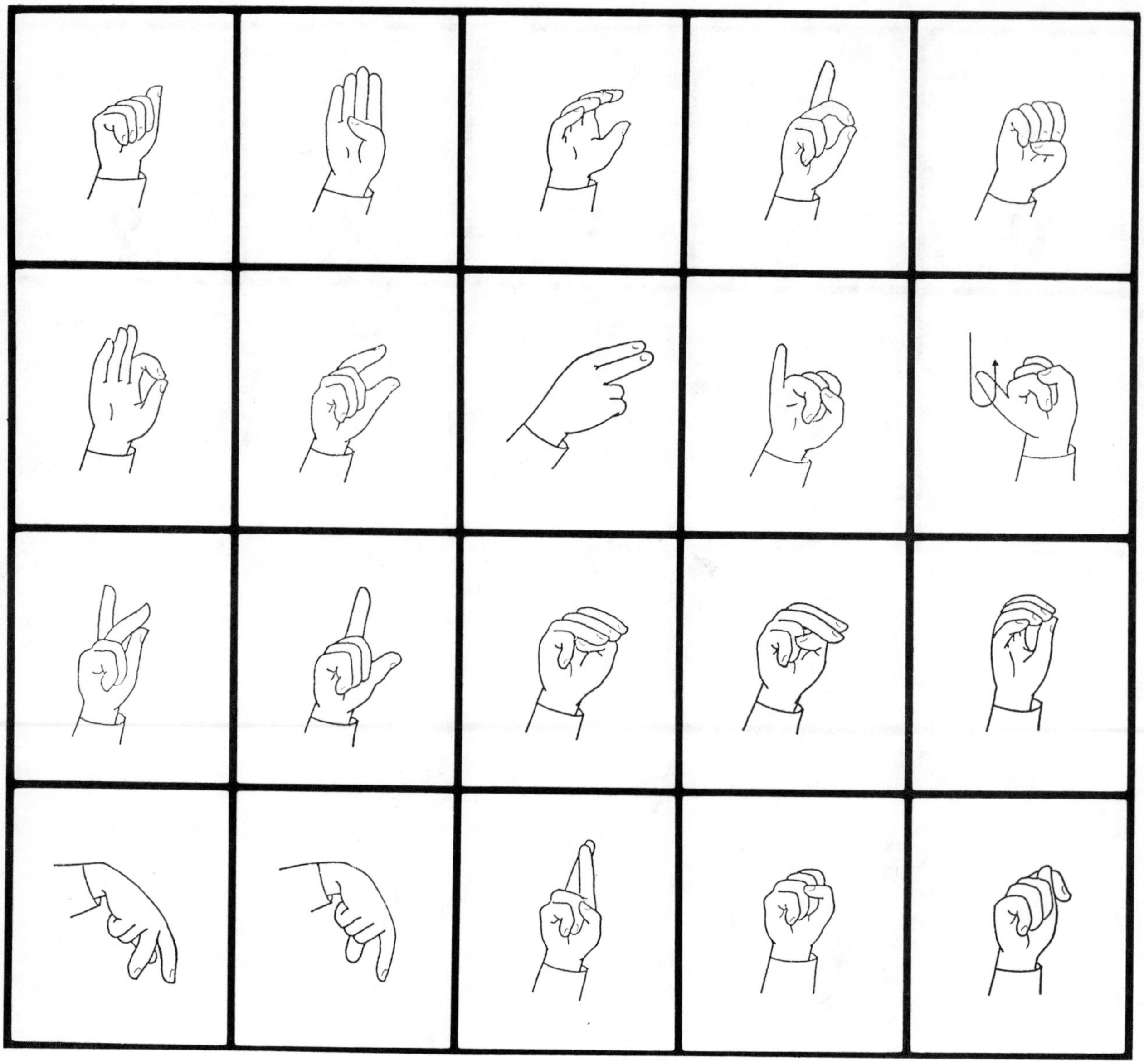

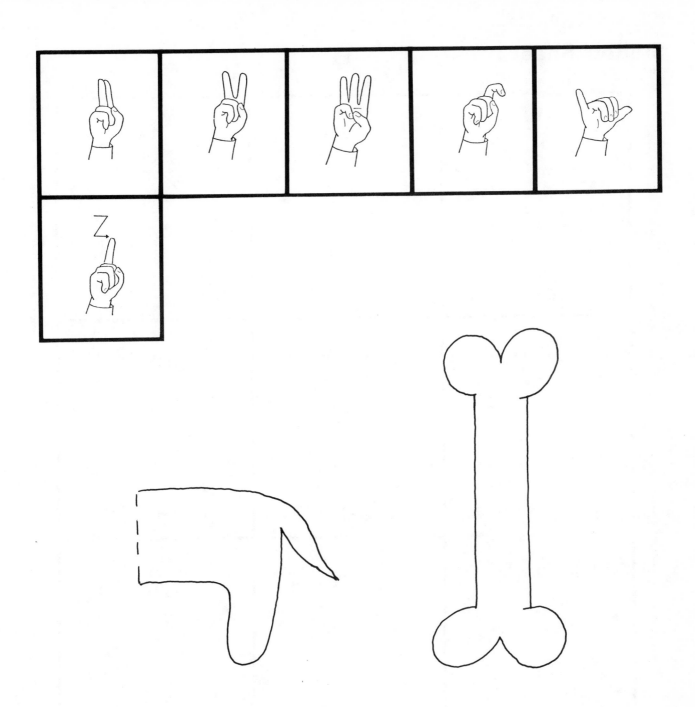

Student Sheet 2

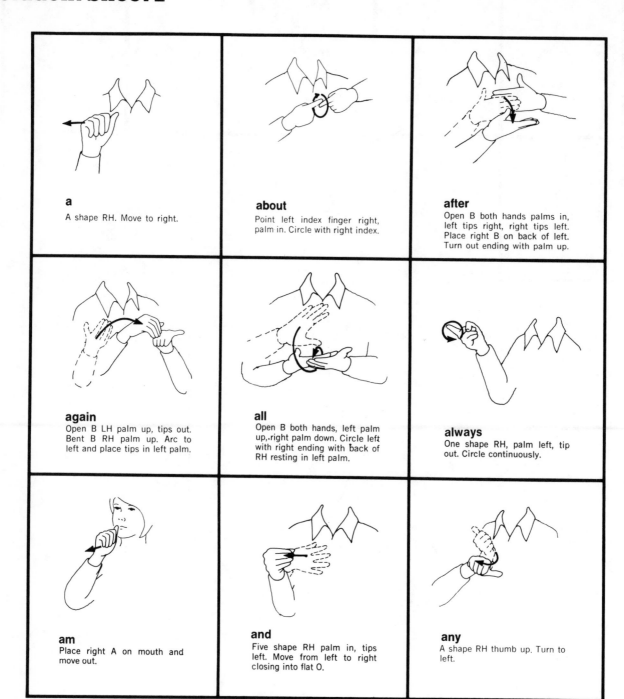

a
A shape RH. Move to right.

about
Point left index finger right, palm in. Circle with right index.

after
Open B both hands palms in, left tips right, right tips left. Place right B on back of left. Turn out ending with palm up.

again
Open B LH palm up, tips out. Bent B RH palm up. Arc to left and place tips in left palm.

all
Open B both hands, left palm up, right palm down. Circle left with right ending with back of RH resting in left palm.

always
One shape RH, palm left, tip out. Circle continuously.

am
Place right A on mouth and move out.

and
Five shape RH palm in, tips left. Move from left to right closing into flat O.

any
A shape RH thumb up. Turn to left.

are
Place right R on lips, then move forward.

around
One shape LH palm in. Circle with right index which is held tip down.

as
One shape both hands knuckles down, tips out. Place index fingers together and move to left.

ask
Palms together tips out. Arc back to body ending with tips up.

at
Touch back of left A with right finger tips.

be
B shape RH palm left, tips up. Place index finger on mouth and move out.

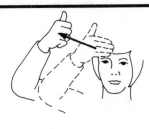

because
Open B RH palm in, tips left. Place tips on forehead and draw back to right ending in A shape, thumb up.

before
Open B both hands palms in, thumbs up. Place RH inside LH and move back toward body.

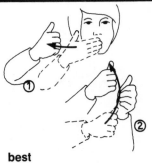

best
A shape LH knuckles right, thumb extended. Place fingers of right open B on lips, bring down in A shape below LH, then brush upward and past LH.

continued

Student Sheet 2—*continued*

better
Open B RH, palm in, tips left. Place tips on chin then move upward into A shape with thumb extended.

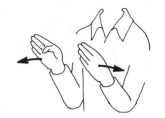

big
B shape both hands, palms facing, tips out. Move away from one another.

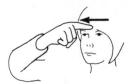

black
Draw index finger across forehead from one brow to the other.

blue
B shape RH palm left, tips up. Shake slightly.

both
V shape RH palm in. Place in left C which is held palm in, then draw down and out.

bring
Open B both hands palms up, one slightly behind the other. Move toward body as if carrying something.

brown
B shape RH palm out, tips up. Place on right cheek and bring down a little.

buy
Place back of right hand in left palm. Lift up and out.

by
Form the letters B and Y in quick succession as if one movement.

call
Place right C at right side **of** mouth and move out.

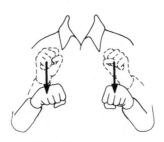

can (verb)
S shape both hands knuckles down. Move down in forceful motion.

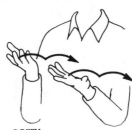

carry
Open 5 both hands palms up, tips slanted left. Move from left to right or vice versa in front of body.

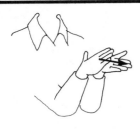

clean
Open B both hands left palm up, tips out; right palm down, tips left. Brush right palm across left as if wiping clean.

cold
S shape both hands. Draw hands close to body and "shiver".

come
One shape both hands knuckles up, tips out. Bring tips up and back toward chest.

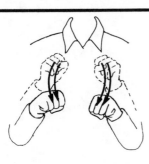

could
S shape both hands knuckles down. Move down in forceful motion. Repeat.

cut
V shape RH palm in, tips left. Move fingers as if snipping with scissors.

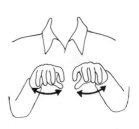

do
Claw shape both hands palms down. Swing back and forth.

continued

Student Sheet 2—*continued*

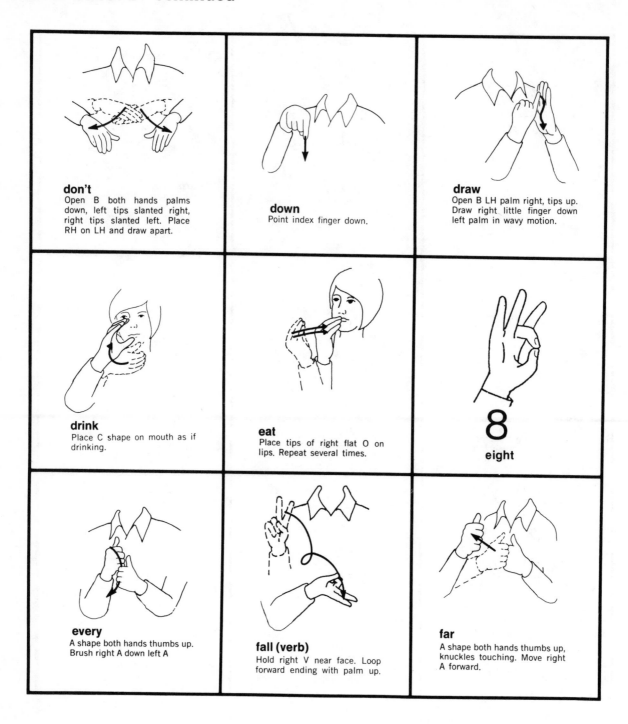

don't
Open B both hands palms down, left tips slanted right, right tips slanted left. Place RH on LH and draw apart.

down
Point index finger down.

draw
Open B LH palm right, tips up. Draw right little finger down left palm in wavy motion.

drink
Place C shape on mouth as if drinking.

eat
Place tips of right flat O on lips. Repeat several times.

8
eight

every
A shape both hands thumbs up. Brush right A down left A

fall (verb)
Hold right V near face. Loop forward ending with palm up.

far
A shape both hands thumbs up, knuckles touching. Move right A forward.

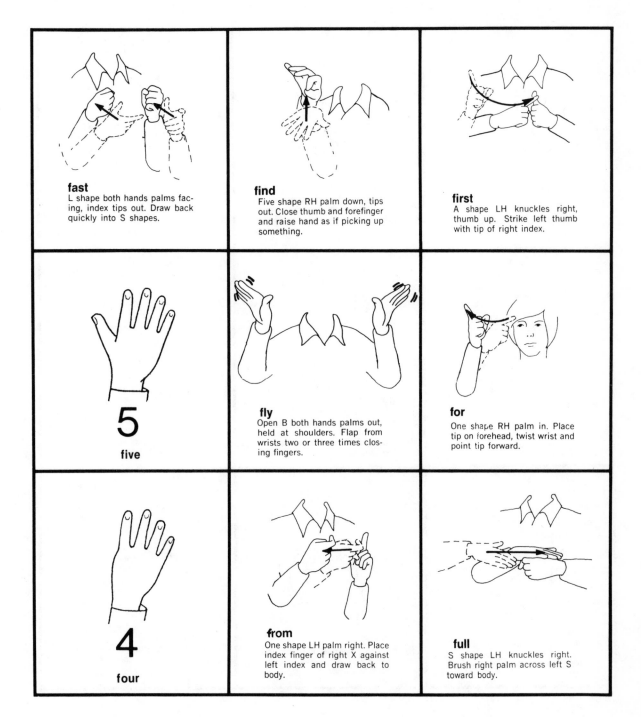

fast
L shape both hands palms facing, index tips out. Draw back quickly into S shapes.

find
Five shape RH palm down, tips out. Close thumb and forefinger and raise hand as if picking up something.

first
A shape LH knuckles right, thumb up. Strike left thumb with tip of right index.

5
five

fly
Open B both hands palms out, held at shoulders. Flap from wrists two or three times closing fingers.

for
One shape RH palm in. Place tip on forehead, twist wrist and point tip forward.

4
four

from
One shape LH palm right. Place index finger of right X against left index and draw back to body.

full
S shape LH knuckles right. Brush right palm across left S toward body.

continued

Student Sheet 2—*continued*

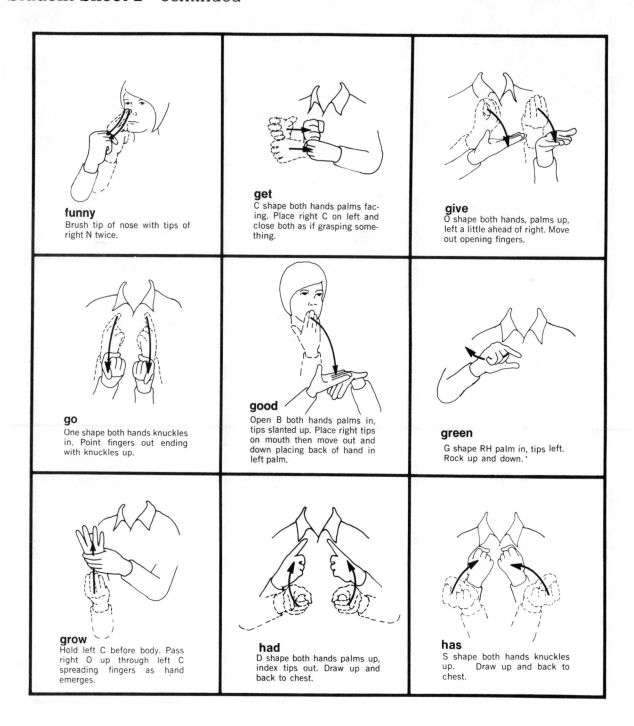

funny
Brush tip of nose with tips of right N twice.

get
C shape both hands palms facing. Place right C on left and close both as if grasping something.

give
O shape both hands, palms up, left a little ahead of right. Move out opening fingers.

go
One shape both hands knuckles in. Point fingers out ending with knuckles up.

good
Open B both hands palms in, tips slanted up. Place right tips on mouth then move out and down placing back of hand in left palm.

green
G shape RH palm in, tips left. Rock up and down.

grow
Hold left C before body. Pass right O up through left C spreading fingers as hand emerges.

had
D shape both hands palms up, index tips out. Draw up and back to chest.

has
S shape both hands knuckles up. Draw up and back to chest.

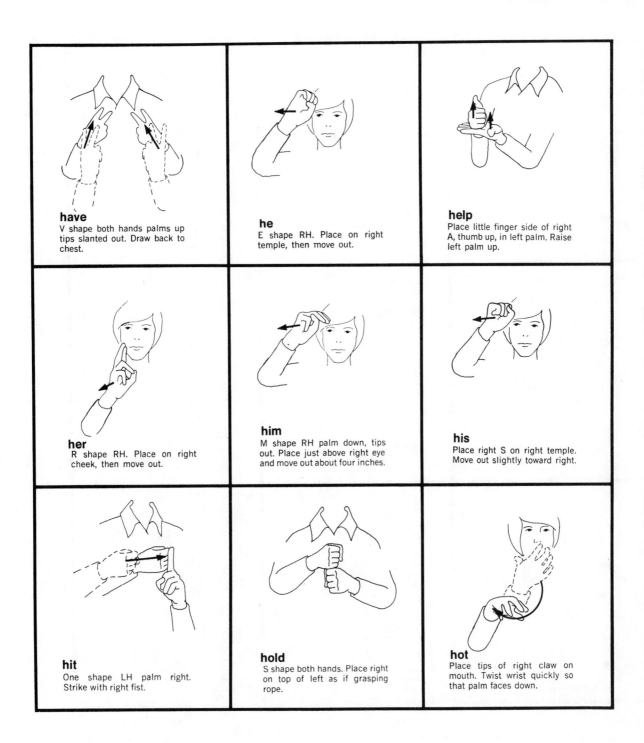

have
V shape both hands palms up tips slanted out. Draw back to chest.

he
E shape RH. Place on right temple, then move out.

help
Place little finger side of right A, thumb up, in left palm. Raise left palm up.

her
R shape RH. Place on right cheek, then move out.

him
M shape RH palm down, tips out. Place just above right eye and move out about four inches.

his
Place right S on right temple. Move out slightly toward right.

hit
One shape LH palm right. Strike with right fist.

hold
S shape both hands. Place right on top of left as if grasping rope.

hot
Place tips of right claw on mouth. Twist wrist quickly so that palm faces down.

continued

Student Sheet 2—*continued*

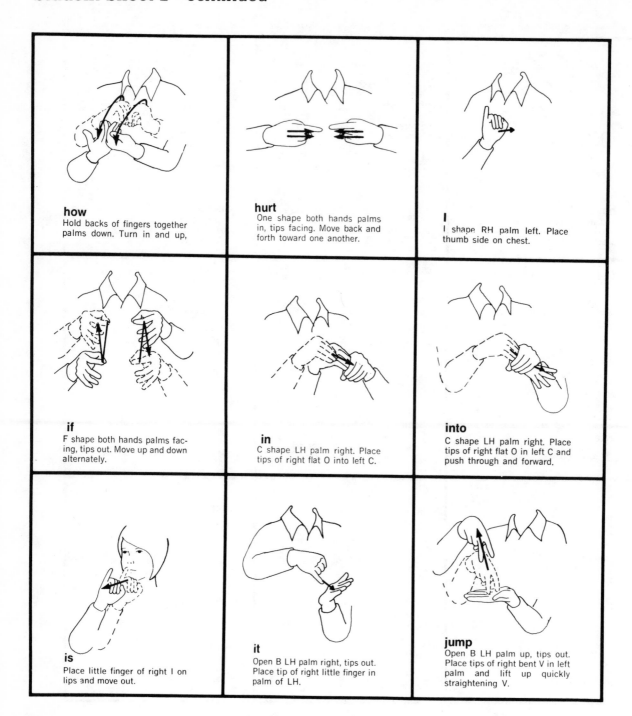

how
Hold backs of fingers together palms down. Turn in and up.

hurt
One shape both hands palms in, tips facing. Move back and forth toward one another.

I
I shape RH palm left. Place thumb side on chest.

if
F shape both hands palms facing, tips out. Move up and down alternately.

in
C shape LH palm right. Place tips of right flat O into left C.

into
C shape LH palm right. Place tips of right flat O in left C and push through and forward.

is
Place little finger of right I on lips and move out.

it
Open B LH palm right, tips out. Place tip of right little finger in palm of LH.

jump
Open B LH palm up, tips out. Place tips of right bent V in left palm and lift up quickly straightening V.

just
Open B LH palm right, tips up. Trace J on left palm with right little finger.

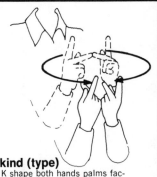

keep
V shape both hands palms facing, tips out. Place right V on left V.

kind (type)
K shape both hands palms facing, middle tips touching. Circle out and around ending with palms in, little fingers touching.

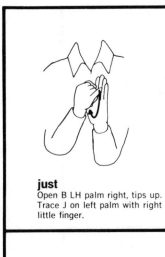

know
Open B RH palm in, tips up. Pat forehead with tips.

laugh
Place index fingers on sides of mouth and move up into A shapes twice.

let
L shape both hands palms facing, index tips pointed slightly down. Bring to upright position.

light
Flat O's both hands fingers back to back. Bring up and spread fingers wide, palms in.

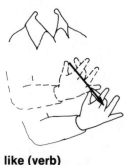

like (verb)
Place right middle finger and thumb on upper chest, then draw out and close fingers.

little
L shape both hands palms facing, index tips out. Move close together.

continued

Student Sheet 2—*continued*

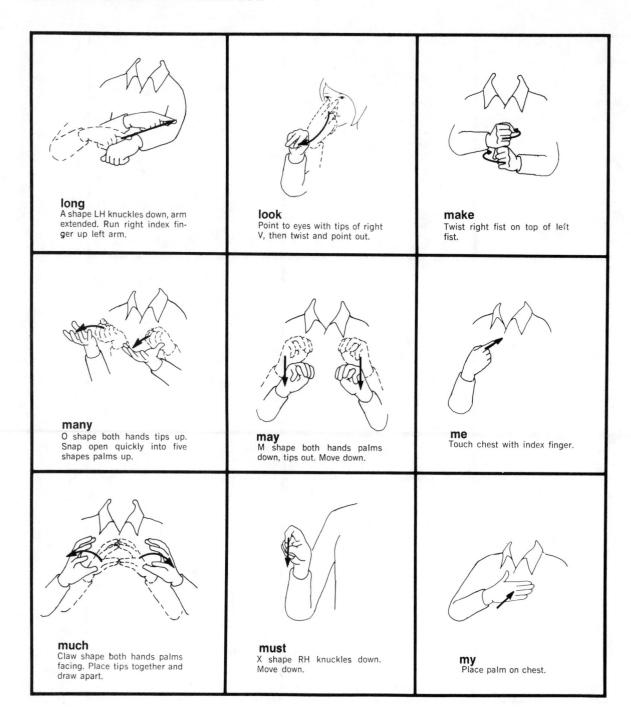

long
A shape LH knuckles down, arm extended. Run right index finger up left arm.

look
Point to eyes with tips of right V, then twist and point out.

make
Twist right fist on top of left fist.

many
O shape both hands tips up. Snap open quickly into five shapes palms up.

may
M shape both hands palms down, tips out. Move down.

me
Touch chest with index finger.

much
Claw shape both hands palms facing. Place tips together and draw apart.

must
X shape RH knuckles down. Move down.

my
Place palm on chest.

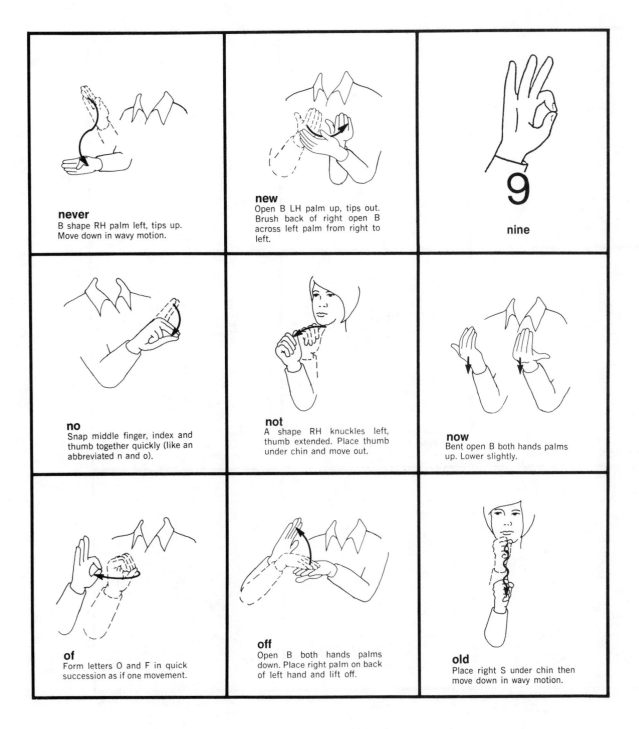

never
B shape RH palm left, tips up. Move down in wavy motion.

new
Open B LH palm up, tips out. Brush back of right open B across left palm from right to left.

nine

no
Snap middle finger, index and thumb together quickly (like an abbreviated n and o).

not
A shape RH knuckles left, thumb extended. Place thumb under chin and move out.

now
Bent open B both hands palms up. Lower slightly.

of
Form letters O and F in quick succession as if one movement.

off
Open B both hands palms down. Place right palm on back of left hand and lift off.

old
Place right S under chin then move down in wavy motion.

continued

Student Sheet 2—*continued*

on
Open B both hands palms down, left tips out, right tips left. Place right palm on back of left palm.

once
Open B LH palm right, tips out. Strike middle of left palm with index tip once.

1

one

only
Hold index finger up palm out. Describe semi-circle counter clockwise, ending with palm in.

open
Open B both hands palms down, tips out, index fingers touching. Draw apart and turn so that palms face each other.

or
Form the letters O and R in quick succession as if one movement.

our
C shape RH palm left. Place thumb just under right shoulder. Circle to left ending with little finger resting just below left shoulder.

out
C shape left hand palm right. Place fingers of right flat O in left C and pull out.

over
Open B both hands palms down, left tips right, right tips out. Pass RH over LH.

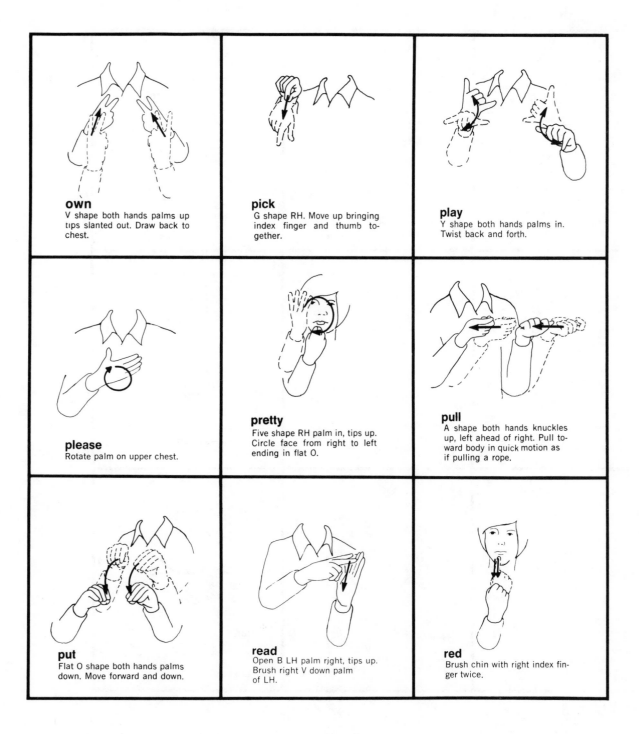

own
V shape both hands palms up tips slanted out. Draw back to chest.

pick
G shape RH. Move up bringing index finger and thumb together.

play
Y shape both hands palms in. Twist back and forth.

please
Rotate palm on upper chest.

pretty
Five shape RH palm in, tips up. Circle face from right to left ending in flat O.

pull
A shape both hands knuckles up, left ahead of right. Pull toward body in quick motion as if pulling a rope.

put
Flat O shape both hands palms down. Move forward and down.

read
Open B LH palm rjght, tips up. Brush right V down palm of LH.

red
Brush chin with right index finger twice.

continued

Student Sheet 2—*continued*

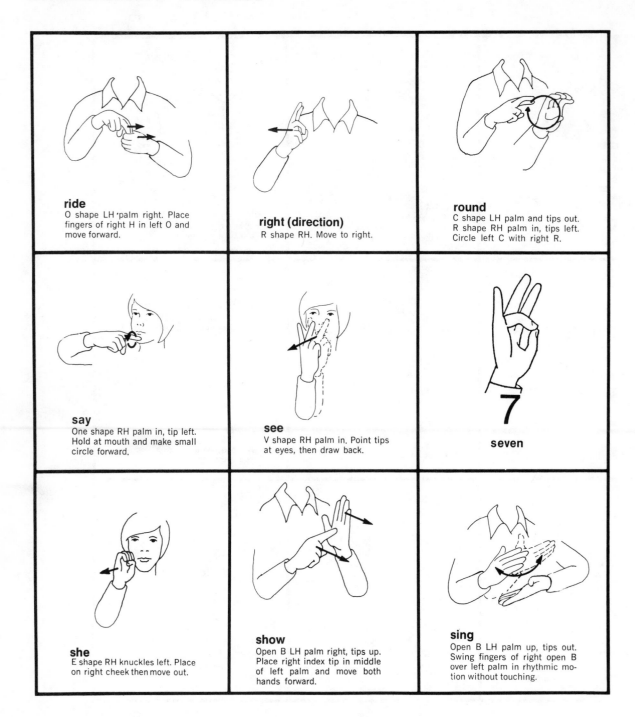

ride
O shape LH palm right. Place fingers of right H in left O and move forward.

right (direction)
R shape RH. Move to right.

round
C shape LH palm and tips out. R shape RH palm in, tips left. Circle left C with right R.

say
One shape RH palm in, tip left. Hold at mouth and make small circle forward.

see
V shape RH palm in. Point tips at eyes, then draw back.

seven

she
E shape RH knuckles left. Place on right cheek then move out.

show
Open B LH palm right, tips up. Place right index tip in middle of left palm and move both hands forward.

sing
Open B LH palm up, tips out. Swing fingers of right open B over left palm in rhythmic motion without touching.

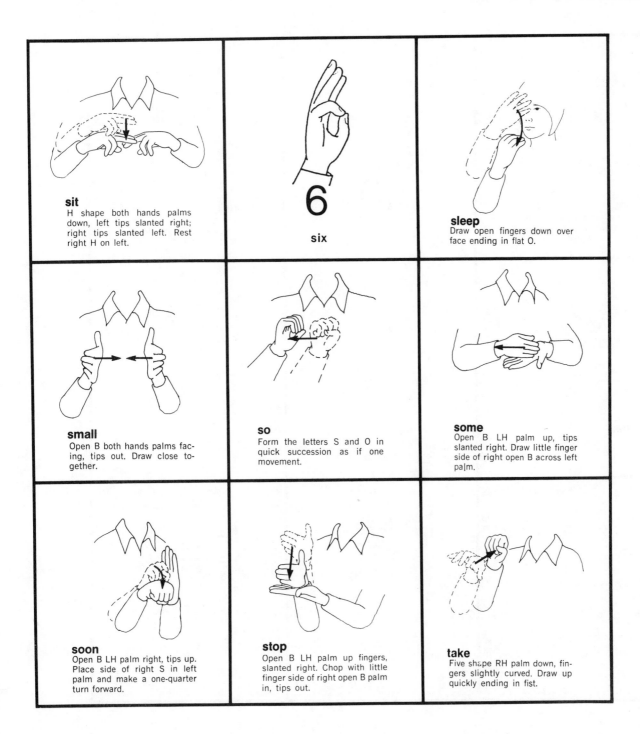

sit
H shape both hands palms down, left tips slanted right; right tips slanted left. Rest right H on left.

six

sleep
Draw open fingers down over face ending in flat O.

small
Open B both hands palms facing, tips out. Draw close together.

so
Form the letters S and O in quick succession as if one movement.

some
Open B LH palm up, tips slanted right. Draw little finger side of right open B across left palm.

soon
Open B LH palm right, tips up. Place side of right S in left palm and make a one-quarter turn forward.

stop
Open B LH palm up fingers, slanted right. Chop with little finger side of right open B palm in, tips out.

take
Five shape RH palm down, fingers slightly curved. Draw up quickly ending in fist.

continued

Student Sheet 2—*continued*

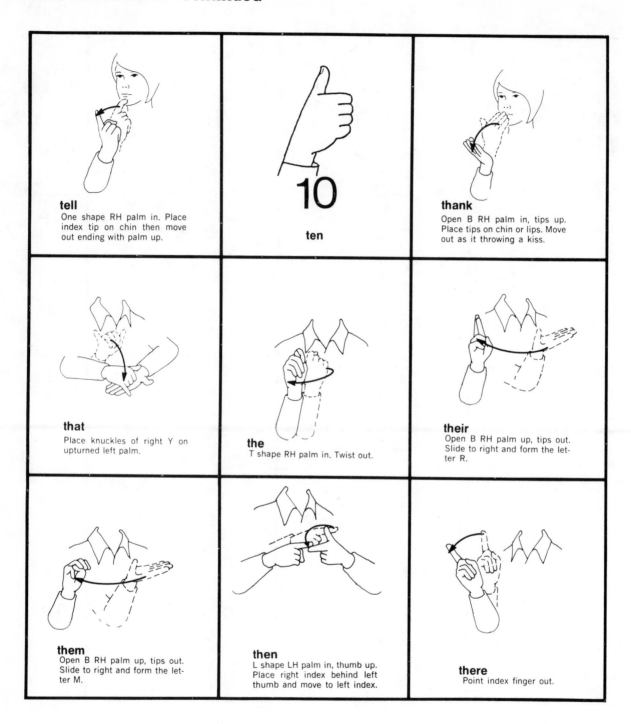

tell
One shape RH palm in. Place index tip on chin then move out ending with palm up.

ten

thank
Open B RH palm in, tips up. Place tips on chin or lips. Move out as it throwing a kiss.

that
Place knuckles of right Y on upturned left palm.

the
T shape RH palm in. Twist out.

their
Open B RH palm up, tips out. Slide to right and form the letter R.

them
Open B RH palm up, tips out. Slide to right and form the letter M.

then
L shape LH palm in, thumb up. Place right index behind left thumb and move to left index.

there
Point index finger out.

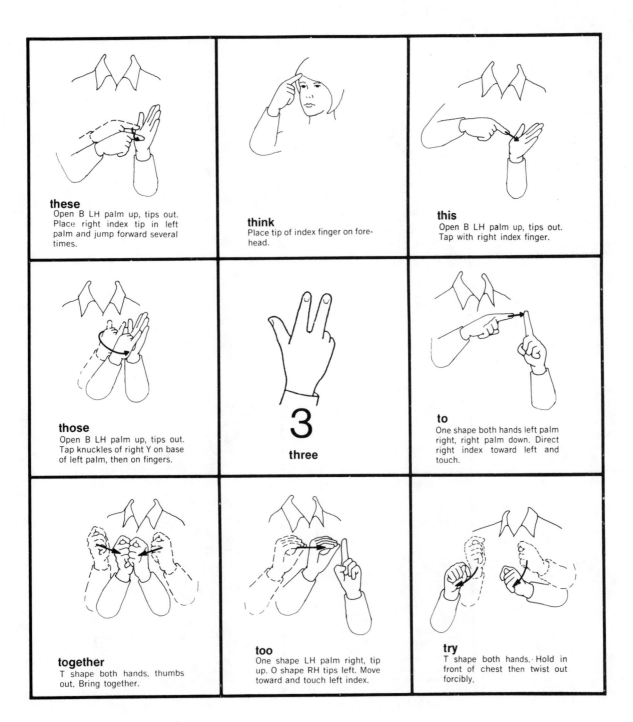

these
Open B LH palm up, tips out. Place right index tip in left palm and jump forward several times.

think
Place tip of index finger on forehead.

this
Open B LH palm up, tips out. Tap with right index finger.

those
Open B LH palm up, tips out. Tap knuckles of right Y on base of left palm, then on fingers.

3

three

to
One shape both hands left palm right, right palm down. Direct right index toward left and touch.

together
T shape both hands, thumbs out. Bring together.

too
One shape LH palm right, tip up. O shape RH tips left. Move toward and touch left index.

try
T shape both hands. Hold in front of chest then twist out forcibly.

continued

Student Sheet 2—*continued*

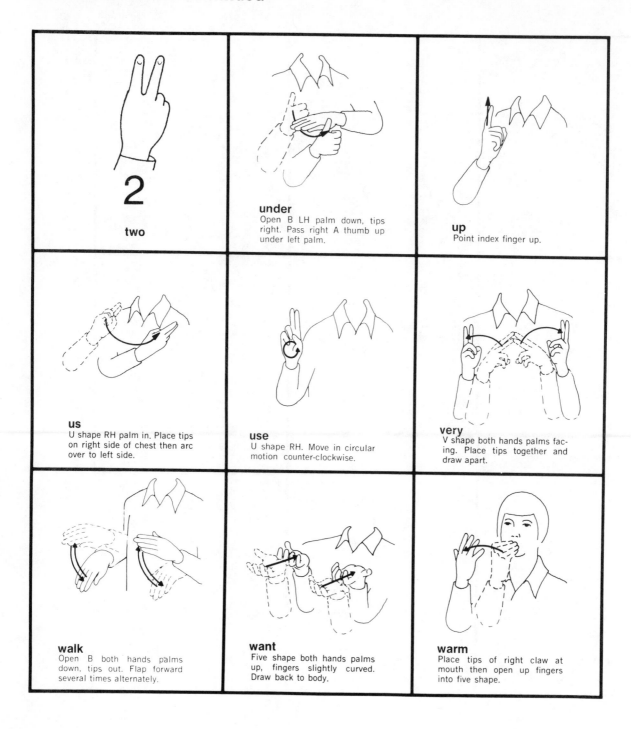

two

under
Open B LH palm down, tips right. Pass right A thumb up under left palm.

up
Point index finger up.

us
U shape RH palm in. Place tips on right side of chest then arc over to left side.

use
U shape RH. Move in circular motion counter-clockwise.

very
V shape both hands palms facing. Place tips together and draw apart.

walk
Open B both hands palms down, tips out. Flap forward several times alternately.

want
Five shape both hands palms up, fingers slightly curved. Draw back to body.

warm
Place tips of right claw at mouth then open up fingers into five shape.

was
Place index finger of right W on lips and move back to right cheek.

wash
Rub right S in circular motion on upturned left palm.

we
Touch right index finger to right side of chest and arc to left.

well (adv.)
Open B LH palm and tips slanted up. W shape RH palm in. Place tips on mouth, then move out and down to left palm.

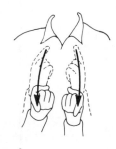

went
One shape both hands knuckles in. Point fingers out ending with knuckles up.

were
Place right R on lips and move back to right cheek.

what
Five shape LH palm up, fingers slanted right. Draw right index tip across left fingers.

when
Hold left index finger up palm in. Circle with right index finger and then touch tips.

where
One shape RH hand. Wave from left to right.

continued

Student Sheet 2—*continued*

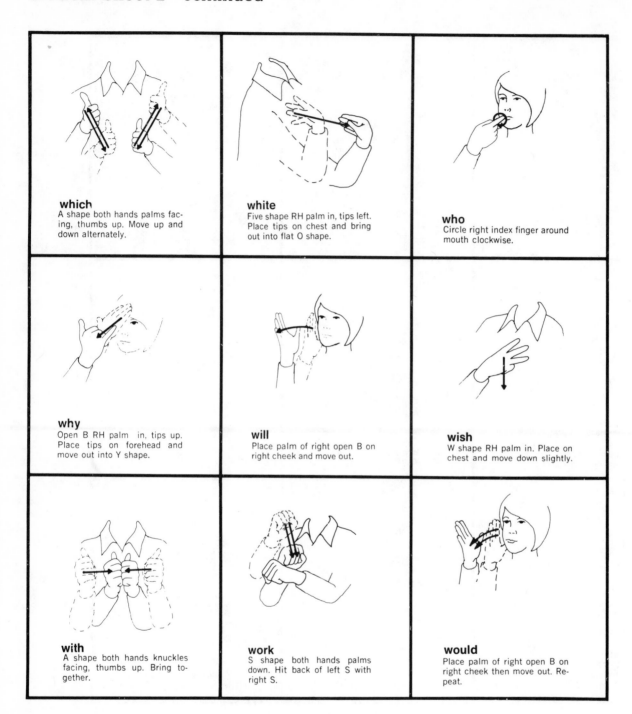

which
A shape both hands palms facing, thumbs up. Move up and down alternately.

white
Five shape RH palm in, tips left. Place tips on chest and bring out into flat O shape.

who
Circle right index finger around mouth clockwise.

why
Open B RH palm in, tips up. Place tips on forehead and move out into Y shape.

will
Place palm of right open B on right cheek and move out.

wish
W shape RH palm in. Place on chest and move down slightly.

with
A shape both hands knuckles facing, thumbs up. Bring together.

work
S shape both hands palms down. Hit back of left S with right S.

would
Place palm of right open B on right cheek then move out. Repeat.

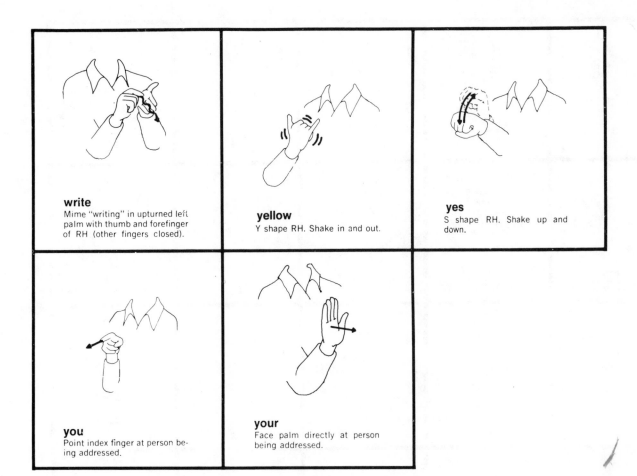

write
Mime "writing" in upturned left palm with thumb and forefinger of RH (other fingers closed).

yellow
Y shape RH. Shake in and out.

yes
S shape RH. Shake up and down.

you
Point index finger at person being addressed.

your
Face palm directly at person being addressed.

Student Sheet 3

A	B	C	D	E
F	G	H	I	J
K	L	M	N	O
P	Q	R	S	T
U	V	W	X	Y
Z				

Student Sheet 4

A	B	C	D	E
F	G	H	I	J
K	L	M	N	O
P	Q	R	S	T

continued

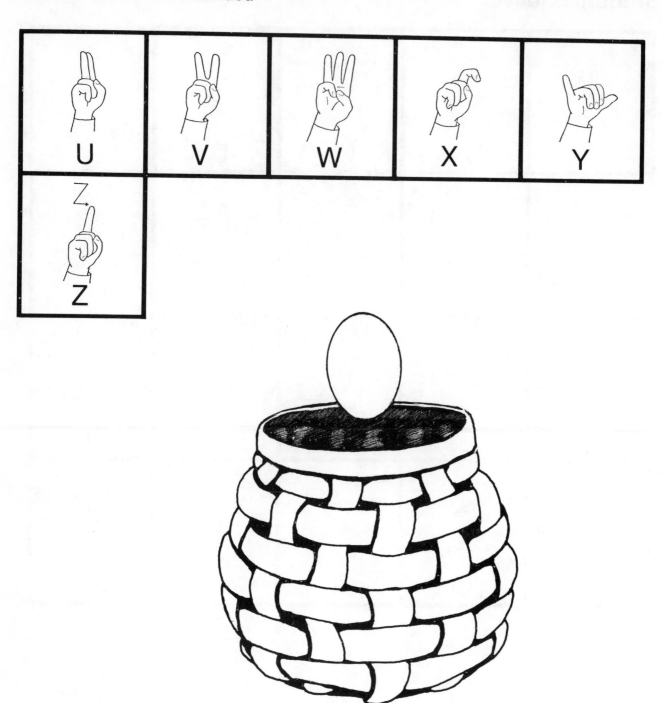

Student Sheet 5

real
One shape RH palm left. Place finger on lips and move up and out.

real
One shape RH palm left. Place finger on lips and move up and out.

real
One shape RH palm left. Place finger on lips and move up and out.

real
One shape RH palm left. Place finger on lips and move up and out.

real
One shape RH palm left. Place finger on lips and move up and out.

real
One shape RH palm left. Place finger on lips and move up and out.

real
One shape RH palm left. Place finger on lips and move up and out.

real
One shape RH palm left. Place finger on lips and move up and out.

impossible
One shape both hands palms down, tips slanted toward one another. Strike tip of left index with tip of right passing on down.

continued

Student Sheet 5—*continued*

impossible
One shape both hands palms down, tips slanted toward one another. Strike tip of left index with tip of right passing on down.

impossible
One shape both hands palms down, tips slanted toward one another. Strike tip of left index with tip of right passing on down.

impossible
One shape both hands palms down, tips slanted toward one another. Strike tip of left index with tip of right passing on down.

impossible
One shape both hands palms down, tips slanted toward one another. Strike tip of left index with tip of right passing on down.

impossible
One shape both hands palms down, tips slanted toward one another. Strike tip of left index with tip of right passing on down.

impossible
One shape both hands palms down, tips slanted toward one another. Strike tip of left index with tip of right passing on down.

impossible
One shape both hands palms down, tips slanted toward one another. Strike tip of left index with tip of right passing on down.

Student Sheet 6

a	a	a	a	a	a	a	a	a	b
b	c	c	d	d	d	d	e	e	e
e	e	e	e	e	e	e	e	e	f
f	g	g	g	h	h	i	i	i	i
i	i	i	i	i	j	k	l	l	l
l	m	m	n	n	n	n	n	n	o
o	o	o	o	o	o	o	p	p	q
r	r	r	r	r	r	s	s	s	s
t	t	t	t	t	t	u	u	u	u
v	v	w	w	x	y	y	z		

Student Sheet 7

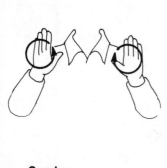

Sunday
Open B both hands palms out.
Circle away from each other.

Monday
M shape RH. Move in small
clockwise circle.

Tuesday
Move right T in small circle.

Wednesday
Move right W, in small
circle counter-clockwise.

Thursday
Circle right H clockwise.

Friday
Make small circle with right F.

Saturday
Move right S in small clockwise
circle.

Student Sheet 8

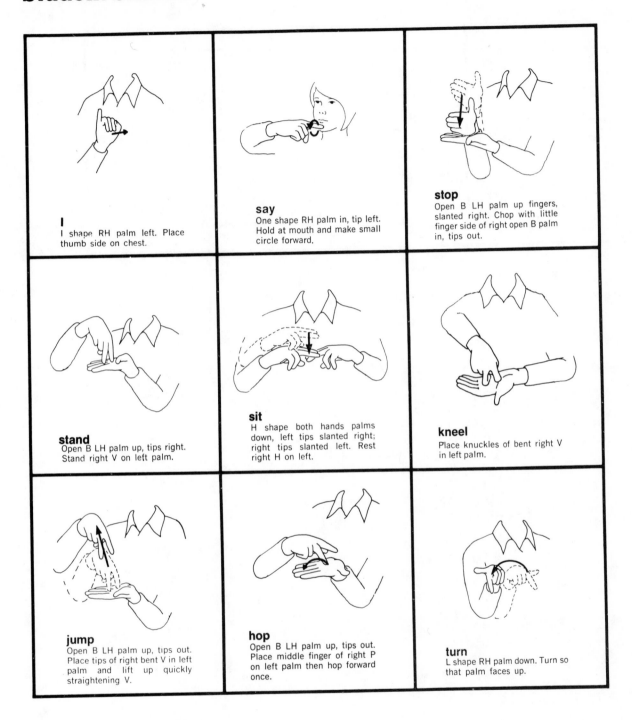

I
I shape RH palm left. Place thumb side on chest.

say
One shape RH palm in, tip left. Hold at mouth and make small circle forward.

stop
Open B LH palm up fingers, slanted right. Chop with little finger side of right open B palm in, tips out.

stand
Open B LH palm up, tips right. Stand right V on left palm.

sit
H shape both hands palms down, left tips slanted right; right tips slanted left. Rest right H on left.

kneel
Place knuckles of bent right V in left palm.

jump
Open B LH palm up, tips out. Place tips of right bent V in left palm and lift up quickly straightening V.

hop
Open B LH palm up, tips out. Place middle finger of right P on left palm then hop forward once.

turn
L shape RH palm down. Turn so that palm faces up.

continued

Student Sheet 8—*continued*

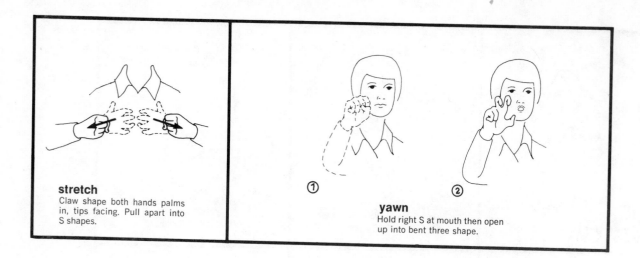

stretch
Claw shape both hands palms in, tips facing. Pull apart into S shapes.

yawn
Hold right S at mouth then open up into bent three shape.

Student Sheet 9

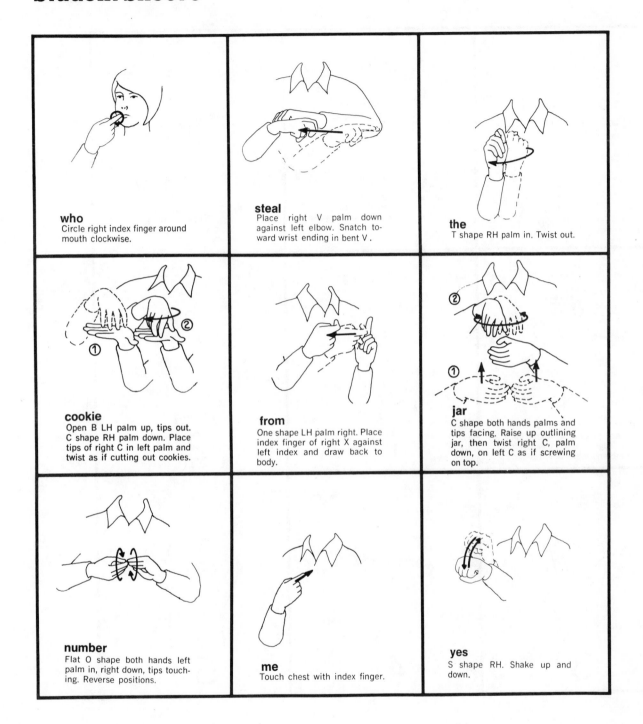

who
Circle right index finger around mouth clockwise.

steal
Place right V palm down against left elbow. Snatch toward wrist ending in bent V.

the
T shape RH palm in. Twist out.

cookie
Open B LH palm up, tips out. C shape RH palm down. Place tips of right C in left palm and twist as if cutting out cookies.

from
One shape LH palm right. Place index finger of right X against left index and draw back to body.

jar
C shape both hands palms and tips facing. Raise up outlining jar, then twist right C, palm down, on left C as if screwing on top.

number
Flat O shape both hands left palm in, right down, tips touching. Reverse positions.

me
Touch chest with index finger.

yes
S shape RH. Shake up and down.

continued

Student Sheet 9—*continued*

you
Point index finger at person being addressed.

can't
One shape both hands palms down, tips slanted toward one another. Strike tip of left index with tip of right passing on down.

be
B shape RH palm left, tips up. Place index finger on mouth and move out.

then
L shape LH palm in, thumb up. Place right index behind left thumb and move to left index.

1

2

3

4

5

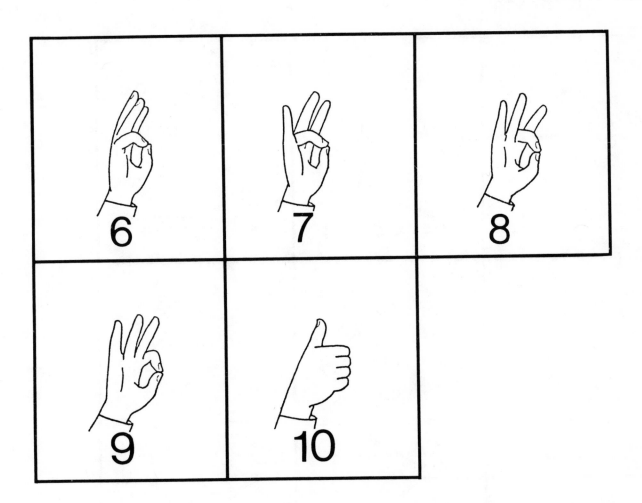

Student Sheet 10

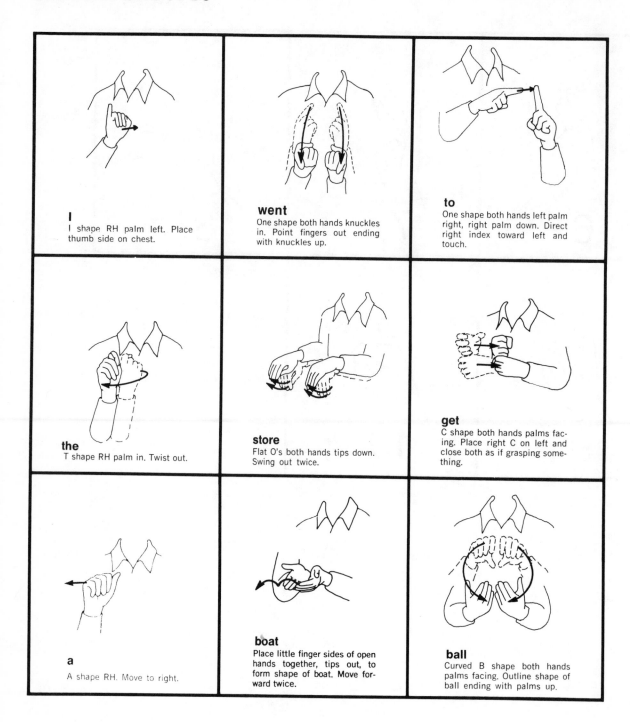

I
I shape RH palm left. Place thumb side on chest.

went
One shape both hands knuckles in. Point fingers out ending with knuckles up.

to
One shape both hands left palm right, right palm down. Direct right index toward left and touch.

the
T shape RH palm in. Twist out.

store
Flat O's both hands tips down. Swing out twice.

get
C shape both hands palms facing. Place right C on left and close both as if grasping something.

a
A shape RH. Move to right.

boat
Place little finger sides of open hands together, tips out, to form shape of boat. Move forward twice.

ball
Curved B shape both hands palms facing. Outline shape of ball ending with palms up.

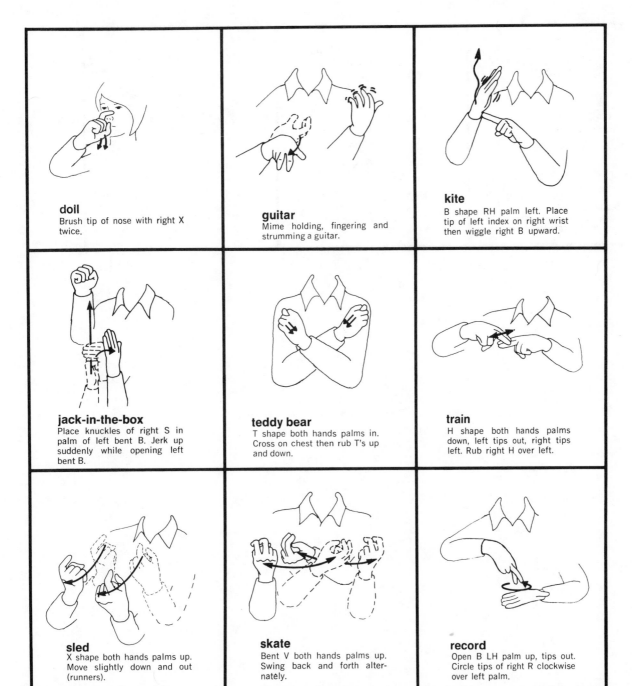

doll
Brush tip of nose with right X twice.

guitar
Mime holding, fingering and strumming a guitar.

kite
B shape RH palm left. Place tip of left index on right wrist then wiggle right B upward.

jack-in-the-box
Place knuckles of right S in palm of left bent B. Jerk up suddenly while opening left bent B.

teddy bear
T shape both hands palms in. Cross on chest then rub T's up and down.

train
H shape both hands palms down, left tips out, right tips left. Rub right H over left.

sled
X shape both hands palms up. Move slightly down and out (runners).

skate
Bent V both hands palms up. Swing back and forth alternately.

record
Open B LH palm up, tips out. Circle tips of right R clockwise over left palm.

continued

Student Sheet 10—*continued*

book
Palms together thumbs up. Open as if opening book.

frisbee
A shape RH palm up. Move quickly to the right opening into five shape.

and
Five shape RH palm in, tips left. Move from left to right closing into flat O.

Student Sheet 11

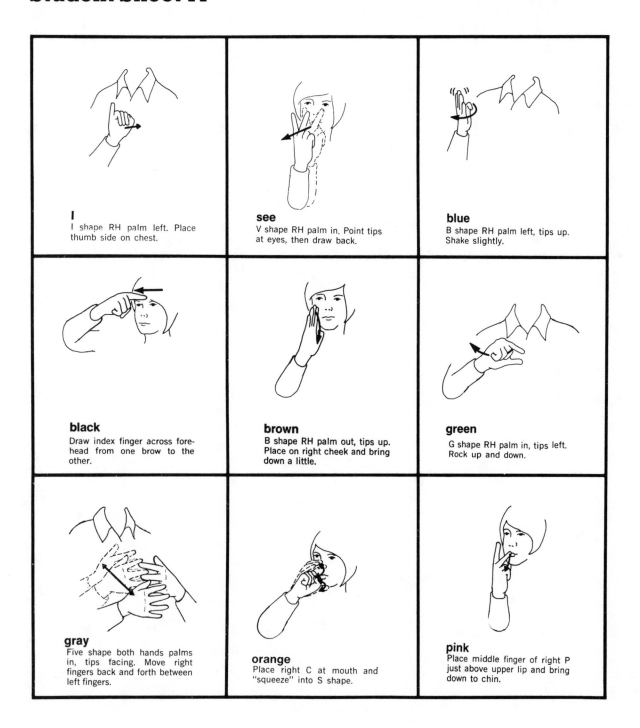

I
I shape RH palm left. Place thumb side on chest.

see
V shape RH palm in. Point tips at eyes, then draw back.

blue
B shape RH palm left, tips up. Shake slightly.

black
Draw index finger across forehead from one brow to the other.

brown
B shape RH palm out, tips up. Place on right cheek and bring down a little.

green
G shape RH palm in, tips left. Rock up and down.

gray
Five shape both hands palms in, tips facing. Move right fingers back and forth between left fingers.

orange
Place right C at mouth and "squeeze" into S shape.

pink
Place middle finger of right P just above upper lip and bring down to chin.

continued

purple
Wave right P back and forth.

red
Brush chin with right index finger twice.

yellow
Y shape RH. Shake in and out.

Student Sheet 12

Dear Parents—

Our class is using total communication in our reading/language arts program. We are combining the use of as many senses as possible because research has shown that is an effective way to learn.

Your child is not only seeing, saying, and hearing words but also *feeling* words. In order to feel words, we are using sign language. Your child is learning a few signs, as needed, during reading/language arts class.

Ask your child to tell you about his or her experiences with seeing, saying, hearing, and feeling words.

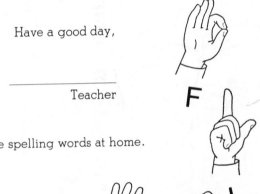

Have a good day,

_____

Teacher

P.S.   Using sign language is a fun, effective way to practice spelling words at home.

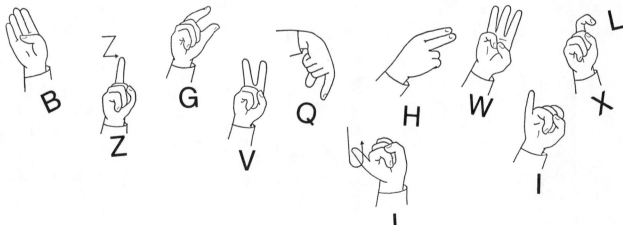

Student Sheet 13

CERTIFICATE OF ACHIEVEMENT

_____ has accomplished the following
(Name)

with the help of Sign Language.

He/she _____

_____

Teacher

Date _____

REFERENCES

Abbott, C. Encodedness and sign language. *Sign Language Studies*, 1975, *7*, 109-20.

Abrams, J. C. Neurological and psychological influence on reading. In H. K. Smith (Ed.), *Perception and Reading*. Proceedings of International Reading Association, 1968, *12*, 4, 63-67.

Asher, J. J. The total physical response approach to second language learning. *The Modern Language Journal*, 1969, *53*, 3-17.

Asher, J. J., Kusuda, J. A., & de la Torre, R. Learning a second language through commands: The second field test. *The Modern Language Journal*, 1974, *58*, 24-32.

Asher, J. J., & Price, B. X. The learning strategy of the total physical response: Some age differences. *Child Development*, 1967, *38*.

Balick, S., Spiegel, D., & Greene, G. Mime in language therapy and clinical training. *Archives Physical Medicine and Rehabilitation*, 1976, *57*, 35-38.

Battison, R. Gesture in aphasic rehabilitation and the lateralization of sign language, 1973. Unpublished paper available from Dr. Robin Battison, Department of Linguistics, Northeastern University, Boston, Mass.

Battison, R., & Markowicz, H. Sign aphasia and neurolinguistic theory, 1974. Unpublished paper available from Dr. Robin Battison, Department of Linguistics, Northeastern University, Boston, Mass.

Bellugi, U., & Klima, E. Two Faces of Sign: Iconic and Abstract. *Origins and Evolution of Language and Speech*. S. Harnad (Ed.), New York: New York Academy of Sciences, 1975.

Bonvillian, J. D., & Nelson, K. F. Sign language acquisition in a mute autistic boy. *Journal of Speech and Hearing Disorders*, 1976, *41*, 339-347.

Bornstein, H. A description of some current sign systems designed to represent English. *American Annals of the Deaf*, 1973, *118*, 454-463.

Brain, L. *Speech Disorders*. London: Butterworths, 1965.

Brasel, K. E., & Quigley, S. P. Influence of certain language and communication environments in early childhood on the development of language in deaf individuals. *Journal of Hearing and Speech Research*, 1977, *20*, 95-107.

Brown, R. Why are sign languages easier to learn than spoken languages. In T. J. O'Rourke (Ed.), *Proceedings of the Sign Language Symposium*. New York: Cambridge University Press, in press.

Charlip, R., & Miller, M. B. *Hand Talk*. New York: Parents' Magazine Press, 1974.

Charuk, J. M. The effects of visual-haptic training on reading achievement. *Dissertation Abstracts International*, 1974, *34*, 9, 5707A.

Chen, L. C. Y. Manual communication by combined alphabet and gestures. *Archives of Physical Medicine and Rehabilitation*, 1971, *52*, 381-384.

Chester, S. L., & Egolf, D. B. Nonverbal communication in aphasia therapy. *Rehabilitation Literature*, 1974, *35*, 231-233.

Creedon, M. P. *Language development in nonverbal autistic children using a simultaneous communication system*. Paper presented by Society for Research in Child Development (Philadelphia, Pa., March 31, 1973). (ERIC Document Reproduction Service No. ED 078 624.)

Denton, D. M. *A Study in the Educational Achievement of Deaf Children*. Proceedings of the 42nd meeting of the Convention of American Instructors of the Deaf, Flint, Mich. 1965, 428-438.

Duffy, R. J., Duffy, J. R., & Pearson, K. L. Pantomime recognition in aphasics. *Journal of Speech and Hearing Research*, 1975, *18*, 115-132.

Fant, L. *Say It With Hands*. Silver Spring, Md.: National Association for the Deaf, 1964.

Ferguson, E. The mind's eye: Nonverbal thought in technology. *Science*, 1977, *197* (4306), 827-836.

Fernald, G. *Remedial Techniques in Basic School Subjects*. New York: McGraw-Hill, 1943.

Fristoe, M. *Language Intervention Systems for the Retarded*. Decatur, Ala.: L. B. Wallace Development Center, 1975.

Fristoe, M., & Lloyd, L. L. *The Use of Manual Communication with the Retarded*. Paper presented at the Gatlinburg Conference on Research in Mental Retardation. Gatlinburg, Tenn., 1977.

Gardner, B. T., & Gardner, R. A. Evidence for sentence constituents in the early utterances of child and chimpanzee. *Journal of Experimental Psychology: General*, 1975, *104*, 244-267.

Glass, A., Gazinaga, M. S., & Premack, D. Artificial language training in global aphasics. *Neuropsychologia*, 1973, *11*, 95-103.

Goodglass, H., & Kaplan, E. Disturbances of gesture and pantomime in aphasia. *Brain*, 1965, *86*, 703-720.

Grinker, R. R., Sr. (Ed.). *Psychiatric Diagnosis, Therapy and Research on the Psychotic Deaf*. Final Report, Grant No. RD 2407 S, Social and Rehabilitation Service, Department of Health, Education and Welfare, 1969. Available from Dr. Grinker, Michael Reese Hospital, 2959 S. Ellis Ave., Chicago, Ill., 60612.

Guillory, L. *Expressive and Receptive Fingerspelling for Hearing Adults*. Baton Rouge, La.: Claitors Publishing Division, 1966.

Hamanaka, T., & Ohashi, H. "Aphasia" in pantomimic sign language. *Study Phonologica*, 1973/1974, *8*, 23-35.

Hestor, M. S. *Manual Communication*. In P. V. Doctor (Ed.), Report of Proceedings of International Congress on Education of Deaf and of 41st Meeting of Convention of American Institute for the Deaf, Gallaudet College, Washington, D.C., pp. 211-221, 1963.

Hoemann, H. The transparency of meaning of sign language gestures. *Sign Language Studies*, 1975, *7*, 151–161.

Hoemann, H. *Communicating with Deaf People: A Resource Manual for Teachers and Students of American Sign Language*. Baltimore: University Park Press, 1978.

Hoffmeister, R. J., & Farmer, A. Development of manual sign language in mentally retarded deaf individuals. *Journal of Rehabilitation of the Deaf*, 1972, *6*, 19–26.

Hofsteater, H. T. *An Experiment in Pre-School Education*, Gallaudet College Press, Washington, 1959, 3(8).

Holmes, K. *Use of Sign Language with a Hearing Child*. Unpublished master's thesis. Western Maryland College, Westminster, Md., 1980.

Jastak, S. W., Bijou, S. R., & Jastak, S. R. *Wide Range Achievement Test*. Wilmington, Del.: Guidance Associates, 1963.

Kadish, J. A neuropsychological approach to the study of gesture and pantomime in aphasia. *The South African Journal of Communication Disorders*, 1978, *25*, 102–117.

Kahn, J. Comparison of manual-oral training with mute retarded children. *Mental Retardation*, 1977, *15*, 21–23.

Kannapell, B. Bilingualism: A new direction in the education of the deaf. *The Deaf American*, 1974, *26* (10), 65–78.

Kelliher, N. Language at their fingertips. *Early Years*, 1980, *10*, 18–20.

Kimura, D. The asymmetry of the human brain. *Scientific American*, 1973, *228*, 70–78.

Klima, E., & Bellugi, U. *The Signs of Language*. Cambridge, Mass.: Harvard University Press, 1979.

Kopchick, G. A., & Lloyd, L. L. Total Communication Programming for the Severely Language Impaired: A 24 Hour Approach. In L. L. Lloyd (Ed.) *Communication and Intervention Strategies*. Baltimore, Md.: University Park Press, 1976, pp. 501–521.

Lake, S. J. *The Hand-Book*. Tucson, Az.: Communication Skill Builders, Inc., 1976.

Lane, H. *The Wild Boy of Aveyron*. Cambridge, Mass.: Harvard University Press, 1976.

Mayberry, R. If a chimp can learn sign language, surely my non-verbal client can too. *ASHA*, 1976, *18*, 223–228.

Meadow, K. Early manual communication in relation to the deaf child's intellectual, social and communicative function. *American Annals of the Deaf*, 1968, *113*, 29–41.

Miller, A., & Miller, E. Cognitive-developmental training with elevated boards and sign language. *Journal of Autism and Childhood Schizophrenia*, 1973, *3*, 65–85.

Mindel, E. D., & Vernon, M. *They Grow in Silence*. Silver Spring, Md.: National Association for Deaf Press, 1971.

Montgomery, G. W. Relationship of oral skills to manual communication in profoundly deaf students. *American Annals of Deaf*, 1966, *111*, 557–565.

Moores, D. F. *Research on manual communication*. Occasional paper 7. Minneapolis, Minn.: University of Minnesota, 1971.

Morozova, N. *Development of the Theory of Preschool Education of Deaf and Dumb*. Moscow: Institute of Defectology, 1954.

Myers, C. A. Reviewing the literature on Fernald's techniques of remedial reading. *Reading Teachers*, 1978, *31 (6), 614*.

Offir, C. W. Their fingers do the talking. *Psychology Today*, 1976, *10*, 73–78.

Premack, D. Language in chimpanzee. *Science*, 1971, *172*, 808–822.

Quigley, S. P. *The Influence of Fingerspelling on the Development of Language*. Communication and Educational Achievement in Deaf Children. Mimeographed report, 1968a. Department of Special Education, University of Illinois, Champaign.

Quigley, S. P. *Deaf Students in Colleges and Universities* (research monograph). Washington, D.C., A. G. Bell Association, 1968b.

Quigley, S. P., & Frisina, D. *Institutionalization and Psychoeducational Development in Deaf Children*. Council for Exceptional Children Research Monograph, Series A, No. 3, 1961.

Reed, J. Aphasia and language function in the deaf. *American Annals of the Deaf*, 1971, *116*, 420–426.

Richardson, T. Sign language for severely mentally retarded and the profoundly mentally retarded. *Mental Retardation*, 1975, *13*, 17–21.

Robins, N., Cagen, J., Johnson, C., Kelleher, H., Record, J., & Vernecchio, J. *Perkins Sign Language Dictionary: A Sign Dictionary for Use with Multiply Handicapped Deaf Children in School*. Watertown, Mass.: Perkins School for Blind (Publication #29), 1975.

Schaeffer, B. Spontaneous language through signed speech. In R. L. Schiefelbusch (Ed.), *Nonspeech Language and Communication: Analysis and Intervention*. Baltimore, Md.: University Park Press, 1980.

Schiefelbusch, R. L. Non-speech Language and Communication: Analysis and Intervention. Baltimore, Md.: University Park Press, 1980.

Segal, E. C. Improving perception through the haptic process. *Academic Therapy*, 1974, *9*, 419–431.

Siger, L. Gestures, the language of sign and human communication. *American Annals of the Deaf*, 1968, *114*, 11–28.

Skelly, M. *Amer-Ind Gestural Code Based on Universal American Indian Hand Talk*. New York: Elsevier North Holland, 1979.

Skelly, M., Schinsky, L., Smith, W. S., Donaldson, R. C., & Griffin, J. M. American Indian sign: A gestural communication system for the speechless. *Archives of Physical Medicine and Rehabilitation*, 1975, *56*, 156–160.

Skinner, B. F. *The Behavior of Organism*. New York: Appleton-Century-Crofts, 1938.

Skinner, B. F. *Verbal Behavior*. New York: Appleton-Century-Crofts, 1957.

Skinner, B. F. *The Technology of Teaching*. New York: Appleton-Century-Crofts, 1968.

Skinner, B. F. *Beyond Freedom and Dignity*. New York: Knopf, 1971.

Stevenson, E. A. *A Study of the Educational Achievement of Deaf Children of Deaf Parents*. Berkeley, Calif.: School for the Deaf, 1964.

Stewig, J. W. I see what you say. *Language Arts*, 1979, *56*, 150–155.

Stuckless, E. R., & Birch, J. W. The influence of early manual communication on linguistic development in deaf children. *American Annals of the Deaf*, 1966, *111*, 452–460.

Topper, S. T. Gesture language for a non-verbal severely retarded male. *Mental Retardation*, 1975, *13*, 30–31.

Vernon, M. Sociological and psychological factors associated with profound hearing loss. *Journal of Speech and Hearing Research*, 1969, *12*, 541–563.

Vernon, M., & Coley, J. D. The sign language of the deaf and reading-language development. *The Reading Teacher*,

1978, 32, *3*, 297–301.

Vernon, M., Coley, J., & DuBois, J. Schooling with sign language. *Instructor*, 1980a, *89*, 42.

Vernon, M., Coley, J. D., & DuBois, J. H. Using sign language to remediate severe reading problems. *Journal of Learning Disabilities*, 1980b, 13, *4*, 46–51.

Vernon, M., Coley, J. D., & Ottinger, P. The use of sign language development process. *Sign Language Studies*, 1979, *22*, 89–93.

Vernon, M., & Koh, S. D. Effects of oral preschool compared to early manual communication on education and communication in deaf children. *American Annals of the Deaf*, 1971, *116*, 569–574.

Vernon, M., & Koh, S. D. Effects of manual communication on deaf children's educational achievement, linguistic competence, oral skills, and psychological adjustment. *American Annals of the Deaf*, 1970, *115*, 527–536.

Walker, N. M. Using the deaf alphabet in language experience exercises. *Journal of Reading*, 1977, *21*, 1–7.

Watson, D. *Talk with Your Hands.* Menasha, Wis.: George Banta Company, Inc., 1964.

Wilbur, R. B. *American Sign Language and Sign Systems.* Baltimore, Md.: University Park Press, 1979.

Zweiban, S. T. Indicators of success in learning a manual communication mode. *Mental Retardation*, 1977, *15*, 47–49.

INDEX

147